THE DEVIL SHOOK MY HAND

I've been shot, stabbed and accused of murder. People call me Britain's deadliest bare-knuckle fighter. This is my story.

MICKY GLÜCKSTAD
WITH MATT NIXSON

JB
JOHN BLAKE

Published by John Blake Publishing Ltd,
3 Bramber Court, 2 Bramber Road,
London W14 9PB, England

www.johnblakepublishing.co.uk

www.facebook.com/Johnblakepub facebook
twitter.com/johnblakepub twitter

First published in paperback in 2012

ISBN: 978 1 85782 799 6

British Library Cataloguing-in-Publication Data:

A catalogue record for this book is available from the British Library.

Design by www.envydesign.co.uk

Printed and bound by CPI Group (UK) Ltd, Croydon, CR0 4YY

1 3 5 7 9 10 8 6 4 2

Papers used by John Blake Publishing are natural, recyclable products made from wood grown in sustainable forests.
The manufacturing processes conform to the environmental regulations of the country of origin.

'This is as I saw it, as I felt it, and I make no apologies for this...'

John Kenneally VC

ACKNOWLEDGEMENTS

Most of the people I've written about in this book are real hard men. You can give them any amount of punishment – long spells in prison, terrible hidings – and pursue them relentlessly through the courts of law, but they'll recover and come back at you time and time again. They'll never stop.

You can never tame them or bend them to your will. That's why they're different from the average man in the street. That's why I'm different, too. We may be a dying breed; we may live outside the rules of normal society and laugh at the petty regulations that keep the ordinary mugs in place. But I firmly believe that if society needed us, if there was another terrible world war for example, all the national heroes would be true hard men.

I want to thank my parents, John and Ivy Glückstad, who inspired me and never faltered in their love and support, even when my actions fell short of their ideals; my brother, John, and sisters, Eileen and Helen, for their acceptance of the parts of my life I did not choose. Thank you.

Additionally, thanks must go to the people who have been there for me every step of the way. Friends like Arnie Fouste, now sadly deceased and deeply missed. His friendship can never be replaced.

Likewise to Dawn Hodges for her support, Patricia Edwards whose encouragement gave me optimism for the future, and to my mates 'Big' Paul Foley and Billy Sprague for their endless loyalty and friendship. A very special mention must go to Danny Woollard for inspiration, and for helping me remember the stories.

And to Billy 'The Fonz' Gibney, for obvious reasons – we both experienced good and bad times growing up in the sixties and no man had a better friend.

Last but not least, a special mention to Gordon Quarry, who I challenged to a fight when I was 16 years old. You won fair and square, putting me on my arse three times. Want to try me now? All respect to you, mate!

I would also like to thank some special former mates whose privacy I will respect by not naming them. Nevertheless, I will always be grateful for the contributions they have made to my life.

So here goes. Hope you enjoy.

CONTENTS

In order to protect identities, many names
and places have been changed.

INTRODUCTION

Micky Glückstad is one of the hardest men in Britain, no argument.

We grew up together in the East End in the fifties and sixties and he has had my back from the day we met. They were tough times but we stuck together and we've never fallen out or fought each other.

Micky's always been a quiet type, not one for bragging or bluster. Anyone who mistakes that for weakness deserves what they get. In his day, Micky was a renowned bare-knuckle fighter and a proper corner merchant, as we called those on the con game. He could buy and sell anything, and he was having people over all the time. He had no scruples. If someone had a few quid and they were greedy and gullible, they were fair game. As a result, he used to get in a lot of fights.

Some of his victims came after him firm-handed and he's been beaten, shot and stabbed on many occasions. He tells people his scarred face is the result of a car accident. But his mates know that each of the scars tells a story. And almost all of his opponents came off worse than he did.

There have been plenty of books about the old East End and the faces who ran it. Hard men such as Roy Shaw and Lenny

McLean have already had their say, and claimed they'd never been beaten. That's not true. Micky Glückstad beat both those men. I was there when he fought Roy Shaw to a standstill. People still talk about the fight to this day. That's why it's time now for him to tell his own story.

The Shaw fight alone, told here for the first time, was a classic. Shaw was the guv'nor then, the best unlicensed fighter in the world. But Micky wouldn't be beaten. He took everything Shaw could throw at him, soaked it up and hit back hard. Quite simply, it was one of the greatest fights I have ever witnessed. The hairs on the back of my neck still stand up thinking about it. Shawy was a mighty man in those days and could have a terrible fight. Micky wasn't doing so well at the time. This was a warm-up: Shawy's promoter Joey Pyle thought Micky would be easy meat before Roy went off to conquer America.

Everyone thought Shaw was going to come out and knock Micky straight into tomorrow. At the weigh-in, Shaw snarled: 'I'm going to do this c**t.' But Micky wasn't having it. He just laughed Shaw off. If I'm honest, I probably thought Micky would have bested Roy on the cobbles, but in the ring the older man would be likely to have the strength, stamina and technique to win.

Roy had been boxing for a long time and training for months. I never saw Micky train for anything. His idea of getting into shape was drinking shorts rather than pints. But he stood his ground like a champion. You have never seen a fight like it, before or afterwards. The crowd was right in the ring with them; everyone was hyped up on adrenalin. It was crazy, a night to be remembered for a long time. But I'll let Micky continue the story. It's his to tell and a good one, too.

Reggie Kray used to say Micky could have been a proper champion if he'd concentrated on boxing, trained properly and kept out of trouble. Reg saw real talent in Micky and only ever had good words to say about him. But he was always a street fighter at heart, and that suited him fine.

A lot of the old faces are dead or live outside London now. They've got big homes in Essex or Kent where they enjoy a comfortable retirement. We've all grown up, settled down and changed. Not Micky. He still lives within a stone's throw of where he grew up. He'll never leave the East End, no matter how much it changes, and it wouldn't be the same without him.

It was always easy come, easy go for him. He was more interested in enjoying himself than in making money and keeping it. But he never let his mates go short either. When he was flush, everyone was flush.

Now you can catch him in a pub, reminiscing about old times. He's got hundreds of stories and they are genuinely incredible. No one has seen or done more than Micky Glückstad. When he told me he was writing a book and asked for my recollections, the memories came thick and fast. I didn't know where to start. But his story gives an insight into a whole generation of men who came from nothing and made something of themselves through hard graft.

Micky knew everyone back in the day, and his experiences shine a real light on a world that probably isn't there any more. I know thousands of people but there is no one I'd rather have watching my back than Micky because he is never going to run out on you – it doesn't matter who you're facing. If you've got a bit of trouble, Micky won't ask who with. He'll ask what time and where you need him, and he'll be there. His friends would do the same for him. When you read this book, you'll see why.

Danny Woollard, January 2012

I first met Micky Glückstad in 1994 when I was living in a flat in Manor Park and having some problems with the landlord, a skinflint old bastard who refused to carry out any work on the property. I refused to pay the rent and Micky was asked by a mutual friend to help get me out of the flat. We later became pals and I learned a great deal about the cornering game from Micky.

If Micky took your money, you lost it for good, and, believe me, he didn't care who you were. Micky always worked alone and taxed many well-known faces. We all bleed the same so why should he care? He even conned me for a few hundred quid when I first met him. That was my first lesson. Micky had been shot three times, stabbed, axed and beaten and left for dead, but he is still alive and going strong.

The man has a stone-cold, no-nonsense attitude and, trust me, he is best pals with the devil. His eyes are emotionless like an English bull terrier, and sometimes you can see his past violence ticking away. If you mess with Micky, he will take you down and still sleep like a baby. Roy Shaw told me himself he wouldn't want a fight on the cobbles with Micky.

There have been a lot of books, but it's about time a real man who has lived a real life in the ruthless and cruel world has the opportunity to put his story forward. That man is Micky Glückstad. In this age of make-believe bullshit, Micky is one man who you don't gossip about to his face. This man shook the devil's hand for sure.

Billy Boy Yates, January 2012

CHAPTER ONE

'I FELT 10 FEET TALL AND SLIGHTLY SHAKY FROM THE ADRENALIN RUSH. IT WAS A FEELING I LIKED. THE OTHER KIDS LOOKED AT ME DIFFERENTLY AFTER THAT – WITH RESPECT AND FEAR. I LIKED THAT, TOO...'

AN EAST END CHILDHOOD

The adrenalin surged through my veins as I strode head down towards the group of lads. They hadn't spotted me in the early-morning gloom of the East London schoolyard. But I'd clocked the four of them, laughing and chatting, their backs turned to me, the moment I came through the old iron gates. Reaching into my pocket, I slowly unscrewed the lid of the Vicks VapoRub and stuck two fingers into the greasy ointment, making sure they were covered, then the other two.

The day before, mistaking my poor English and my Norwegian surname for signs of weakness, my four antagonists had threatened me with a kicking unless I handed over my dinner money. Having arrived back in London a week earlier after six months abroad, I looked and sounded different to the other kids and stuck out like a sore thumb to the bullies.

They'd sneered at me: 'Glückstad, that's a funny name. You're a flash little git too. We want your money tomorrow.'

It was a shilling in 1959 but I swore instantly that they weren't getting a penny. I learned their names as I walked away from the confrontation, heart pounding. Michael Collins, Mike Eid, Steven Sawyer and Billy Gibney – the school toughs. 'We'll be waiting for you tomorrow, Glückstad,' Collins called after me. 'You'd better not mess us around.'

I went home that night and never told my mum. I didn't want to worry her. My sister Eileen and I had only just arrived back in London from Oslo. My dad – who was Norwegian, hence the surname Glückstad – had thought it important for us to get to know our family and its roots on the other side of the North Sea. Bringing up four kids on the breadline in post-war London was hard on Mum too, so she reluctantly agreed. It would give her a much-needed break.

We were put on a ship and sent to stay with Dad's sister, Alget. The crossing took two days in rough seas. I puked my guts up every time I tried to eat and the ship's engines echoed through the steel hull at all hours of the day and night like never-ending thunder. We bunked in a small cabin in the bowels of the vessel and watched in astonishment as our meagre possessions vibrated backwards and forwards across the floor in time to the booming of the screws. Much later, when I was in prison, I imagined myself back on the ship escaping England, my cramped cell our cabin.

Norway was a world away from the claustrophobic, chaotic and noisy East End we'd left behind. London was bombed-out buildings, gas lamps and big shire horses pulling the carts for the breweries down dirty, potholed streets. The sky seemed permanently dark and a dusting of soot covered everything, washed away briefly only when it rained. By contrast, Oslo was clean and modern. Aunt Alget lived in a big wooden house 50 miles or so south of Oslo in Fredrikstad and was well off by our standards. She was part owner of the *Oslo Gazette*, the local paper, and moved in influential circles. We were received warmly and lived happily amid a large and generous group of aunts and uncles, and my grandmother, a lovely lady who was reputed to have been the oldest person in Norway when she finally died at the ripe old age of 106. In contrast to austerity England, we had plenty of food and good clothes and went to a small school where we were soon speaking pidgin Norwegian and making new friends.

It was an idyllic existence for two scruffy working-class kids from the East End. Acres of open space to play in, trees and fields everywhere, and a loving, safe environment away from the bomb sites and unexploded munitions that still littered London. Maybe my life would have turned out differently if we had stayed. I don't remember it ever being suggested. Eileen and I missed our mum and loved our younger siblings, John and Helen, but, like all youngsters, we were easily distracted, and forgetting our old lives was easy.

When we did return I was nearly 11 years old and growing fast into a strong young man, having bulked up on the plentiful Norwegian food. Now, more than 50 years on, I can still feel the excitement as our ship docked in Tilbury and we ran down the gangplank into Mum's arms. I had to learn English all over again but we were home and the entire family was together again.

My father John had married my English mother, Ivy, after meeting her by chance at Charing Cross station during the dark days of 1943 when they were both on leave from war work. He was a Norwegian merchant seaman whose ship helped smuggle downed Allied airmen back to England and resistance fighters into occupied Norway – a bit like the Kirk Douglas movie *The Heroes of Telemark*.

Mum was serving with the Women's Auxiliary Air Force. They literally bumped into each other, and got talking. Well, Dad didn't speak much English but they ended up going for a meal and they later told us kids it was love at first sight. After that, they met whenever their work allowed it, which wasn't often, and married as soon as the war ended. Despite the fact that his family was overseas and Norway had been liberated, Dad agreed to make his home with Mum in London.

I was born in Plaistow in the East End of London five years after that chance meeting, on 4 May 1948, the second of four kids, on the first floor of a big old rented house with gas lamps and a coal fire. The Second World War had ended three years before but the bomb sites and wreckage from the pounding Hitler's bombers had given the East End during the Blitz remained. All around were broken buildings and shattered people trying to rebuild their city and their lives.

These days, you can't imagine just how bad the poverty and destitution we suffered were. But for us kids, the wreckage provided a ready-made adventure playground. Climbing down into bombed-out cellars and making dens in the ruins, we traded pieces of shrapnel and played our own version of war with sticks for guns and stones for grenades. Spent bullet cartridges could still be found amid the rubble and were prized above all else. We collected them obsessively and swapped them among ourselves. But even as kids, we saw that everything was old and dirty and tired. London was like a knackered old girl who'd had the stuffing knocked out of her.

The rag and bone man still came down our street calling out for pots and pans, and everything we owned was second-hand and patched over patches. The milkman, the coalman and the breweries, Watney's and Charrington's, still used horse-drawn carts to deliver their wares and we would run out when they passed, fighting off the other kids to grab the manure for Mum's tiny vegetable patch. London must have been unique in that, when it rained, it seemed to get dirtier rather than cleaner.

As for us, we barely had a pot to piss in, but, despite our poverty, we were never short of love and have remained a close family to this day. Mum would stoke the embers of our open fire and toast bread and crumpets using a long fork as we gathered round of an evening. We had five chickens in the backyard – each of us had our own favourite – and fresh eggs supplemented our diet until food rationing finally ended in 1954, and we ate our feathered friends one by one. Every Sunday, Mum would get a big tin bath out and, when the weather was fine, we'd carry the boiling water from the communal hob out into the yard. When it was full we'd bathe one at a time and then Mum would use the water to wash our clothes. Afterwards, I'd help her by turning the handle of a rusty old mangle to ring the soapy water from the sopping clothes.

When we weren't at school, we used to scrounge empty orange and banana boxes from Queen's Market in Upton Park. We'd chop them up to make small bundles of firewood to sell for kindling during the winter months. The market was a natural gathering place for the gangs of youngsters who roamed the neighbourhood. Some of them had left school at 14 and were working on the stalls. They used to call themselves the Square Boys. Most wore cheesecutter caps pulled down low over their ears against the cold, whistled at passing girls and liked to think they were tough guys. Unlike us, they were proper tearaways, a right handful, always up to mischief and thieving and being chased by the police.

One day my brother Johnny came home with a cut lip. He had been walking through the market with a friend when a ginger lad had stolen his cap and beaten him. I was a big lad with an air of confidence, so the market boys never bothered me. Dad was away at sea most of the time so I had never had anyone to run to. If my brother or sisters were in trouble they'd come to me and I'd try to work out what to do. I relied on my own steam. I wouldn't back down even as a kid. If you were born in those post-war years life was hard, full stop. There weren't many silver spoons about and you had to get on with it. I was very protective of my siblings and knew it was up to me to uphold our family pride in the absence of my father.

Ginger, who was four or five years older than me and burly from shifting the crates of fruit and veg, and two of the Square Boys were sitting on an empty stall sharing a fag and looking like the Artful Dodger and his gang from *Oliver Twist*.

'Oi,' I shouted at the lads. 'Why don't you try me for size? I'm not as easy to beat as my brother. You fucking bullies.'

Ginger jumped off the stall, telling his grinning mates: 'Stay out of this, boys, I'll do Glückstad on my own.'

Before he could look back at me I'd floored him with a left hook. But – fair play – he got up again and we beat seven bells out of each other while the other lads gawped. We were that evenly matched, and neither of us would back down. Finally, with both of us exhausted and bleeding, someone suggested a truce and we shook hands on it. Ginger told me his name was Johnny Hunibals and from then on all the market boys were as good as gold. We had a lot of respect for each other and they were always trying to get me involved in their wild schemes, robbing drunks or ambushing other gangs from the area. It was my first fight and I had learned to be fast and aggressive.

While Dad was still at sea, Mum used to clean people's steps to earn a few extra bob. She'd see us off to school and then do her rounds – brushing off the dust and blacking the steps with polish until they shone. She was fiercely proud and it was demeaning work for a respectable woman who had served as a WAAF. Like many ordinary women who had been given a glimpse of work normally reserved for men during the war when they were away fighting, she struggled to return to the more mundane life of an East End housewife. But she had a growing family and she would have done anything to keep body and soul together and her kids in shoes. I hated seeing her going out to work like that for families with money. It made me furious to watch my beloved mum swallow her pride and break her back for us kids.

My father came home every four or five weeks, so we didn't see him much until I was 12 or 13. Dad was a big man who struggled with his English and didn't say a lot but I loved him all the same. When I was still small he'd pick me up on his shoulders and race around the house while I screamed with delight and the other kids chased us. Other times, we'd sit at the table as he built model boats from bits of scrap wood he'd picked up. I remember watching enthralled as he whittled masts and funnels with a small pocket knife.

Almost everyone was up to something in those days. Life was hard for working-class people like us. We lived in ghettos and many broke the law to put food on the table. The police weren't there to protect us; they were there to keep us in line. There may well have been coppers walking the streets like the friendly Dixon of Dock Green played by Jack Warner in the long-running TV series, but if there were we never met them. The Old Bill we came across were more likely to give us a clip round the ear for cheek than a kindly talking-to. People didn't see buying stolen goods or black-market cigarettes as wrong, but as just a necessary way of life. Many run-of-the-mill families kept home and hearth together and a roof over their heads through occasional, though no less illegal, petty crime.

My parents were proud. They would rather have starved than brought shame on themselves and the Old Bill to our door. Our clothes were hand-me-downs and Mum battled to put three meals a day on the table. We would steal fruit from the stalls, or shoplift nuts or matches, and never tell Mum where they came from because she'd make us take them back. We understood their pride, but we also knew how poor we were, so we justified our thieving among ourselves. As the oldest boy, with Dad away so much, I quickly learned to look after my family and myself.

My nan and granddad lived upstairs from us. Granddad Alfred told stories of his brother, Tug Wilson, who had lived in nearby Stratford and worked as a docker. Dead now, he had been a very hard man and contested many bare-knuckle brawls for money. Because I was big for my age and had the makings of a fighter, Granddad encouraged me to shadow-box in a mirror. He'd shout encouragement from his ratty armchair as I ducked and dived in the front room, copying the moves I'd seen the older boys making down the market when they sparred among themselves.

'Always protect your face,' he told me. 'Because you're big, there will be other lads who will be able to move faster than you. So you've got to be clever. You've got to take the punishment as well as dishing it out.'

Sucking hard on his pipe, he'd continue: 'You'll never win if you can't soak it up just as well as you can serve it up. Son, never forget, if you let one single person walk over you, everyone will. Remember that or you'll have to learn it the hard way.'

I never forgot his advice and it was ringing in my ears as I crossed the yard at Whitehall School in Forest Gate, heading for the bullies who had threatened me for my dinner money. I knew instinctively that I couldn't give it to them or they would demand more and I'd be tormented mercilessly from then on. But I wasn't sure about taking all four of them on at once either. To even the odds, I'd stopped off at the corner shop for a jar of Vicks on the way to school. When we had colds Mum made our eyes sting slathering it over our chests to clear our lungs. Once when Eileen had got some in her eyes, she'd cried with pain, tears streaming, until it was washed out, leaving them bloodshot and sore. That had got me thinking.

Collins was the biggest so he would be first. I patted him on the shoulder, then shoved my Vicks-covered fingers into his eyes as he turned round, instantly bringing him to his knees, screaming in pain. The strong menthol stung fiercely, blinding him, and he collapsed, tears pouring down his mug. Now it was three against one. Before the others could react, I punched Gibney straight in the face, feeling his nose crack under my fist. I knew it was a good blow because he crumpled immediately, the fight knocked out of him. I expected the other two to jump me at any moment – I could almost feel a fist in the back of my head – but, with Collins writhing in agony and Gibney dazed and bleeding on the floor, they had lost any stomach for a fight.

'It's nothing to do with us, Glückstad,' said Sawyer, raising his hands as he backed away.

'Just keep out of my way then,' I snarled.

Giving Gibney a boot in the stomach for good measure, I picked up my satchel and headed into class. I felt 10 feet tall and slightly shaky from the adrenalin rush. It was a feeling I liked. The other kids looked at me differently after that – with respect and fear. I liked that, too.

Collins ended up in hospital but never grassed me up and we all became friends. They wanted me to join their fledgling firm. But I didn't want to be in a gang; I didn't need one. I never looked for trouble, although somehow it always found me. I got in a fair few brawls after that at school, always with older boys who fancied themselves as hard men, but I never lost. Mum and Dad got used to me coming home with a shiner or a cut lip or a torn and bloodied shirt. 'I fell over again, Mum,' I'd lie through my teeth.

Billy Gibney, in particular, was to become a lifelong friend who stood shoulder to shoulder with me on many occasions. He introduced me to his other mates: Mike Tucker, Big Terry Holden and Arnold Fouste. Arnie, as we called him, was the easiest bloke to get on with and never stopped talking. Everyone liked him. Later Billy was nicknamed 'The Fonz' after his idol Henry Winkler from the TV series *Happy Days*, and we had many scrapes together before he lost himself to drugs and booze. But back then we stuck to each other like glue.

Billy and I lost our virginity to an older girl a few years later. We'd moved to a larger flat in Forest Gate. I didn't really fancy her but everyone said that she knew what she was doing and I wanted to learn. The rumours were not wrong, but afterwards she told her brother and he told their mum and I got arrested. I was 13 or 14 and she was 15 or 16 but the officers thought I was older because I was big for my age. I stood before the juvenile court for the first time shaking with nerves. The case was kicked out but I was fined £5 for costs, a lot in those days. And given a stern talking-to by the magistrate, a posh bloke in a pinstriped suit who looked at me like something he'd found under a rock. It was my first brush with the justice system. I told Mum the girl was the one who had shown me what to do. She believed me but still gave me a proper clip round the ear. Dear old Mum.

I'd been at Whitehall School for a year when Dad came off the ships. He felt he needed to be at home more, and assert some parental authority. He looked for work on the Royal Docks in nearby Silvertown, both then major employers of East End men. It was hard going because he was a foreigner and didn't have good English. The Cockneys had all the best jobs sewn up but he eventually found work with a shore gang helping unload cargo from all over the globe. England was still the centre of the trading world in those days and hundreds of ships arrived every day.

That summer I was sent back to Norway. Dad could see the company I was keeping – the school tearaways were now firm friends – and he didn't like it. Still, it was good to see the family and I visited an uncle who had a holiday home in Sweden. By East End standards this practically made me Alan Whicker. People didn't travel back then, before the era of cheap flights and foreign holidays. My middle-class relatives could see a change in me. I was coarser, wilder, more out of control. So after four months I was back in Blighty. Wherever I went from then on, I would always return home to the East End.

When I was 14 I got my first tattoo. In those days you could be inked, no questions asked, as long as you had a letter from your parents. First time round, me, Billy Gibney and Mike Eid all had Indian braves done on our right legs as a symbol of friendship. Later I used the same forged letter, with the date carefully changed, to get permission for a tattoo of Jesus on my chest that I became well known for when I was fighting. I was never religious. I just liked the image of Christ on the cross and it looked stunning. It cost 30 bob at Ben Gunn's tattoo parlour in Chingford, about £1.50 in today's money, and I admit it hurt like hell.

I've carried it with me as a guardian angel ever since. I've survived some right old scrapes, been shot three times, and stabbed, slashed and glassed on too many occasions to recall, but I've always come through. My dad, who, unusually for a seaman, had one simple design on his arm, saw my tattoos as a sign of a growing estrangement from my family and their way of life. I protested but it was true. I was drifting further away from them and into delinquency.

One day, after I'd given a little too much lip to one of my teachers, the teacher tried to smack me. I ducked and belted him one in the mouth. I was taken before the headmaster, expelled from Whitehall and sent to another school two miles away. I was gutted to move away from my pals but there was an exciting new crowd at Harold Road School in Upton Park, near West Ham FC. Glen Dixon was my first mate there and introduced me to his pals, who included three black lads: Lenny Riley, Tony Camron and Frank White. In those days, blacks were still a rarity in London and I had a fair few brawls sticking up for them. Even as a boy, I never liked racists. It didn't seem right to judge someone by the colour of his skin and I hope I never have. They were good mates and watched my back more times than I can remember.

It was the time of the Cuban Missile Crisis and rising international tension. In London, people were marching to protest against the threat of World War Three, but in the East End life went on. We had bomb drills in school, when we all climbed under our desks and placed our hands over our eyes. We treated it as an excuse to mess about, but the teachers were deadly serious.

Another time, I remember the air-raid sirens, a relic from the Second World War, going off. Their eerie wailing sound sent the adults running into the street. It was a test, but it scared my parents. Having said all that, surviving life was a daily struggle and most ordinary people just didn't have time to worry about nuclear Armageddon. Memories of the Blitz remained strong and no one believed it could happen again. When President Kennedy was on TV, he might have been from a different planet with his suntan and American accent. For us working-class East Enders, life went on.

Every day I walked two miles from home to class, passing St Bonaventure's Catholic School on the way. Three lads in particular – Paul Foley, Danny Woollard and Jimmy Tibbs – were the local faces or hard boys and I soon knew them to say hello to. I never heard any of them starting a fight or picking on anyone. Yet, like me, they all had formidable reputations for standing up for themselves if pushed too hard. 'Big' Paul especially was known as a promising young boxer and was always trying to get me down the gym for some proper training. But it was another talented amateur, Johnny Clark, who first persuaded me to get into the ring.

We were living in a three-bedroom maisonette over Woolworth's, and Johnny, whose older brother Jimmy was already making waves as a talented amateur boxer, lived two doors down. Johnny wanted to follow in his brother's footsteps and was training at the Double R club in Bow Road, East London.

He kept badgering me to come and keep him company and hone my skills. Eventually I agreed, mainly to keep him off my back. From then on, twice a week after school, I'd jump on the trolley bus past the old Bryant and May match factory and up to Bow. It was to be my introduction to the shady world of backstreet boxing and some of the most famous faces of the era.

CHAPTER TWO

'I COULDN'T SLEEP A WINK, EXCITEMENT, NOT FEAR, KEEPING ME FROM GETTING MY HEAD DOWN. I KEPT REPLAYING THE INCIDENT OVER AND OVER. THE MOMENT THE TEACHER HAD GONE DOWN AND THE CHEERS OF THE OTHER KIDS. IT HAD BEEN THE BEST MOMENT OF MY LIFE...'

JUVENILE DETENTION

It stank of sweat and aggression but the Double R club was about as glamorous a hangout as existed for a cocky 15-year-old who fancied himself a fighter. It had been a derelict office building until Reggie Kray snapped it up for next to nothing. That was while his brother Ron was inside for three years for stabbing a young man and telling the police his blood-soaked clothes were the result of a 'nose bleed'. They didn't believe him. The front room was turned into a bar and club with a large gym on the empty first floor at the back. It had been opened by Henry Cooper in 1957.

Downstairs attracted a mix of celebrities, villains and wide-boy businessmen in sharp suits and wide ties. *Carry On* star Barbara Windsor was among the regulars. Upstairs, an entire wall was mirrored and stacks of weights and pads were piled around the gym. Three or four heavy punch bags hung from the ceiling and the showpiece in the centre of the room was a boxing ring. Just being there was magical. At one point or another, the club was used by just about every half-decent London fighter of that era hoping to achieve their dreams. Boxing then was like football now, a way for ordinary working-class kids to haul themselves out of poverty. Only crime was as popular a way of escaping humble roots. Some, like me, followed both.

I trained at the Double R for nearly a year, honing my technique, learning to punch fast and sharp and to duck my opponent's blows. I also learned how to soak up punishment in the ring and wear an opponent down, so much so that I was often picked as a sparring partner by far better technical fighters because I could stand their blows. Afterwards, Johnny and I would have an orange juice at the bar and from time to time chat to the owner.

In those days Reggie was slightly built, not very tall, and polite to everyone – a softly spoken man who didn't need to shout or throw his weight around. He'd been a promising young boxer himself, turning pro at 16. Then he was jailed for assaulting a policeman before he was out of his teens. That killed his career. So, with brother Ron, he turned to making money through crime. Being on nodding terms with him was a big deal for us. We admired Reggie for making something of his life. In return, Reg always had time to ask how our boxing was going and would often pop into the gym to chew the fat with one of the trainers. Reg knew his own and liked being around hard men. There was a lot of loyalty both ways.

Reg was famous for his cigarette punch. He'd offer his intended victim a fag and, when the unsuspecting man accepted, he'd belt him in the mouth. Because the jaw was loosened around the cigarette, it was easier to break. We used to talk about it in the gym but I never saw Reg in action.

Johnny and I drifted apart soon after that and our lives took very different turns. He never fulfilled his dreams of boxing professionally. Instead, he went into television, working under a pen name as a scriptwriter on some of the most famous shows of the seventies – *The Sweeney*, *The Professionals* and *Z Cars* to name a few. I suppose he must have put those early experiences with us to good use.

Meanwhile, I had left school aged 15 and taken a job delivering newspapers. In reality, I spent most of my time in Len's Café in Forest Gate drinking tea and hanging out with Billy Gibney and my other pals. The windows were permanently steamed up and dripping, which suited the regular customers, and it stank of fried food and cigarettes, but it was our social club and base. My sister Eileen had also left school and was going about with an older boy, Billy Neal. He came from a close and well-known East End family and introduced me to his brothers, Johnny, a stonemason, and the oldest brother, Roy. He was a real hard nut, friends with the Krays, the gangster Charlie Richardson and Jimmy Herring, a local jazz singer.

Roy and Jimmy were close pals and had only recently been released from prison following the death of a local gangster who had tried to run Forest Gate. Murder charges were eventually reduced to manslaughter at the Old Bailey, when they convinced the judge it had been a fist fight that had got out of hand and that they had never meant to kill the bloke. They got six years in the end and I idolised them for standing up to a well-known toerag who had made life a misery for a lot of people. When they told me you couldn't trust a man until you'd served time alongside him, I swallowed every word like it had come down from Mount Sinai with the Ten Commandments via Sunday school.

I was a cocky little so and so, and was soon running errands for them – delivering notes, buying fags or keeping a lookout for the Old Bill when they were up to no good. In return, they gave me cigarettes and a few bob here and there. The entire café mob were 'at it', up to something, and all good money-getters. The most important lesson I learned from them was that nine-to-five jobs were for mugs. They ducked and dived, earning where and when they could. Stolen goods; illegal gambling; selling iffy cigarettes up West; the con game, or cornering as it was known: you name it, they were into it. As long as people wanted new TVs, cars, jewellery, blokes like that would be around to supply them, almost always second-hand!

Crime is a thin line, which you usually cross in only one direction, but they never thieved from their own. There was a simple code of honour among villains. If someone stepped out of line or went too far, they would be given a slap and a talking-to. The second time it would be a proper hiding. After that, there was no telling. That was why men like the Kray Twins wielded so much influence. They kept the balance of power on the streets because they knew everyone and everyone knew them. They were respected because they were fair and many a family in need received a brown envelope to get them to the end of the month or see off the hated council rent collector.

Watching Dad come home knackered from another back-breaking 12-hour shift on the docks, it was no surprise I chose to become a conman. I was never good at school. I was instinctively smart, but like a lot of working-class boys in those days I had no time for learning. I couldn't wait to get out and make my way in the world. I had dreams of boxing inspired by my granddad – and the respect it would earn me – but not the discipline to put my back into proper training. Life as a docker like my dad lacked the glamour of my new mates. They were flush and swanked around in sharp suits, dined out in restaurants and attracted women. I wanted what they had and knew a life slaving my guts out on the docks wasn't going to get it for me, no matter how much overtime I put in.

It was during this time that you could say the devil shook my hand, put his arm round me and welcomed me into his fold. I was not evil. Don't make that mistake. I knew right and wrong. I'd nothing against the fuzz back then, but there were shades of grey. Call me a Robin Hood if you like, but when I became a villain I hope I never went after anyone who couldn't afford it, or didn't deserve it, and I shared my spoils with friends and family. When I was flush, everyone was flush.

Professional criminals are never in it for the money. Well, not entirely. We want the respect of those who subscribe to our mantra and the prestige that being successful in a hard man's world brings. Call us old-fashioned; call us dinosaurs if you like. You might get a smack in the mouth but you might also be right. There was a code of conduct in those days. We were hard but fair and we didn't pick on the weak. You might say we were the ultimate rebels. Britain was still regimented and the class system ruled us with a rod of iron. A lad like me from a poor East London background could struggle for years and still be crushed. The establishment existed to keep us in the gutter where we belonged. Men like the Krays were shaking things up, moving in the same circles as the showbiz elite and royalty. They hadn't let their East End roots stop them building an empire and making them rich, and neither would I. Soon I was swanning about like a young Al Capone.

In truth, despite my ambitions, I was strictly small time, but I would never back down from a fight against anyone and won respect while taking some ferocious hidings. On more than one occasion I stayed away from home with friends, hiding from Mum and Dad until the bruises had gone down.

We were always looking for birds. Always bragging about our conquests. And lying through our teeth about how far we'd got. We'd go anywhere to try to pull. Some weeks I'd be like a lovesick teenager over some girl who'd batted her eyelashes at me over a cup of tea. Then I'd meet someone else and forget about her in seconds. Like money, girls were easy come, easy go from the start. You do all the graft, get stuck in, then they're gone and you're back to square one.

When a roller-skating rink opened in Forest Gate, we sensed it could be fruitful territory for meeting women. Skating was still relatively new to Britain. Everyone wanted to try it and roller rinks were popping up everywhere. It was cheap too, comparatively, so always good for a laugh when we were broke. Despite skating on thin ice many times, I never mastered the art. One afternoon, Billy Gibney, Arnie Fouste and I were having a go.

While my mates zoomed about like experts, I was more interested in trying to catch the eyes of some of the groups of office girls. One girl in particular, a gorgeous brunette with long hair and great legs, attracted my attention. I was a cocky little sod, good looking enough and thought I was God's gift. Whether she noticed me before I went arse over tit and through the crash barriers to howls of laughter from a group of girls on their works outing I'll never know. Someone did though. That was it; I decided to sit out the rest of the afternoon and catch my breath. I had a huge blister, too. Boxing was a man's sport; skating was I didn't know what.

I'd taken off my skates and was minding my own business when a big Irish fella skated up without warning and aggressively demanded to know what I'd been looking at. Not him for sure, and I told him so. Maybe he was the brunette's boyfriend? I didn't have a chance to find out. He was boozed up and looking for bother and had a bunch of mates waiting on the sidelines for muscle. Fuck it. I wasn't looking for bother, not today. He looked a right mug balancing on his skates, trying to be threatening and not slip over all at once. I laughed in his face, hoping he'd fuck off.

'Are you laughing at me?' he snarled.

'Fuck off, mate. Get back to your skating,' I replied.

'You little mug. I wouldn't waste my time on you.'

'What did you say?' I asked.

'You heard me. Now go to fuck.'

That was it. I saw red. Leaning forward I shoved him hard in the chest, then sat down again as he went scrabbling backwards on to his arse across the polished concrete floor. I was pissing myself laughing as he scrambled towards me on his hands and knees, screaming blue murder.

'I'll fucking kill you, so I will.'

My quiet afternoon was shot to hell. I didn't get up; didn't need to. I whacked the muppet straight in the mouth with the heel of my foot, breaking his jaw and bursting his nose like an overripe tomato. He collapsed face down, a rapidly growing pool of claret staining the surface of the rink.

Within seconds, the skating rink had degenerated into total chaos. Girls screaming, men shouting and punters landing in heaps as the bloke's mates piled in, sliding over each other in their eagerness to knock lumps out of me. Worst of all, the brunette had disappeared. Boots, fists and skates were flying everywhere. I couldn't stop laughing. I'd taken a few punches and was in danger of getting a kicking when Arnie steamed in, swinging a skate by its laces, its heavy metal wheels doing plenty of damage. The bouncers had piled in, so we did them as well.

I can still remember one of them standing between the doors and me. He was kicking at me like a donkey, trying to bring me down, frightened to mix it like a man. So I belted him in the nuts, whoof, and smacked him one as he hit the floor clutching his sack in both hands. Billy was punching left and right as we grabbed our shoes, kicked open the fire exit and ran for it. There must have been 25 angry blokes chasing us, some still wearing their skates. It was like something out of the Keystone Kops. Arnie's car was parked round the corner. We jumped in and screamed off. I sat waving cheekily from the back seat and blowing kisses.

Later, we discovered that the lads we'd tangled with called themselves the Canning Town Gang. They had a fierce reputation for fighting and didn't take any prisoners. Most of them ended up behind bars at one time or another, mainly for crimes of violence and dealing drugs. We didn't give a damn. I was all for going tooled up to teach them a proper lesson, but wiser heads won the day.

'They're not worth it, Mick,' said Arnie. 'You gave that big bastard what he deserved. They won't want to mess with us in a hurry.'

'You're right, mate. Cheers.'

The violence I'd dished out added to my growing reputation in Forest Gate and the older lads came to trust me. I was a little soldier, loyal and unquestioning. Work was hard to come by – Britain was still flat broke – but the spivs in Len's Café didn't seem to notice. We all lived well. Not millionaires but not starving. Cars were increasingly common down the East End as well as up West. When we needed a motor, we'd take turns to rob one. A bendy piece of metal would open the door, and then we'd hot-wire the ignition. When we needed money we'd work at whatever scam was going, sometimes even doing a bit of honest graft when there was nothing else about. When we were flush, we'd cruise around drinking, trying to meet women. We might have been small-time villains but we acted like big shots. Nothing scared us.

One day we were sitting in Len's when my brother John came in crying. His teacher, a right bully, had belted him round the face, telling him: 'You're just like your brother – a waste of space.'

Putting my arm round John, I warned him: 'Don't tell Mum or Dad – I'll sort this out for you.'

As ever, Billy came with me and we stormed back into Whitehall School for the first time since my expulsion. The teacher looked shit-scared.

'Get the hell out of here, Glückstad,' he yelled at me as I barrelled across the classroom, hate in my eyes and anger in my heart.

Too late, mate. I nutted him and he went out like a light just as another member of staff came running in, to be met with a right hook from Billy and cheers from the kids. They might have fancied themselves educated but we'd taught them a lesson they'd not get from university. Full of ourselves, we strutted out of the school and back to Len's Café for more tea.

An hour later the local bobbies turned up in force and charged us with actual bodily harm before locking us up overnight. Sitting in that police cell, hungry and cold, I scratched my name in the chipped cream paint with my fingernail: 'Micky G woz here'. I couldn't sleep a wink, excitement, not fear, keeping me from getting my head down. I kept replaying the incident over and over. The moment the teacher had gone down and the cheers of the other kids. It had been the best moment of my life.

Next day at West Ham Magistrates' Court I was too shattered to care what happened. Mum wept and pleaded for clemency for her boy. I'd only been standing up for my brother, she told the magistrates. Billy's parents said the same. The teacher I'd butted gave evidence from behind two black eyes and what looked like half a roll of cotton wool shoved up his nose. The magistrates had us pegged as thugs no matter how respectable our parents were and our feet barely touched the ground. We were given three months apiece and hustled into a Black Maria.

As I was marched past Mum by two enormous coppers, she grabbed me and hugged me tight. 'Be strong, son, and God will keep you,' she whispered in my ear before I was dragged away.

'Thanks, Mum. I'm sorry,' I blurted out.

Even as a non-believer, this turned out to be the second-best bit of advice, after Granddad Alfred's warning against dropping my guard. Billy and I were taken to Ashford, Kent, where we were held overnight before being bussed to Kidlington Detention Centre in Oxfordshire the next day.

The journey was a long one as the coach toured all the juvenile courts and police stations, picking up the kids who had been remanded. Some were sobbing to themselves; others made a show of defiance. I honestly didn't give a damn. The smarmy, bullying teacher had got what he deserved. Of course I felt bad for Mum and Dad; I knew they felt I'd let them down. Well, sod it. No point crying over spilt milk, as Granddad used to say to me. I sat back to enjoy the ride with a smug grin that I thought made me a man.

That grin lasted about as long as it took to process Billy and me. The reform school was a hard place in 1963, even for a tough working-class kid like me who fancied himself as a bit of a bruiser. We were quickly stripped of every last vestige of ourselves. There would be no individualism in Kidlington. Off came everything. All our personal possessions went into bags, to be returned upon our release. You're not allowed to talk to anyone while you're being processed. Herded into ice-cold showers, we stood naked and embarrassed in front of hard-nosed screws who had seen it all before. One of the lads was coughing hard under the cold water. I didn't dare look for fear of catching the eye of the guards. A naked man is defenceless. One who is cold and shivering before the screws is doubly so. It was all part of the process of damping our rebellion. Showing us we were worthless cogs in the machine. Ten minutes before I had been Micky Glückstad. Now I was simply a number and a surname. That number would follow me through the system from day one.

A damp towel was flung at me and I patted myself down quickly. Our clothes were replaced with prison-issue underwear, socks, rough shirts and trousers – all grey, all itchy and all uncomfortable – and rough army surplus blankets for our beds in the dormitory. No privacy, no luxuries, piss-poor food, everything done at double-quick time and the screws screaming at you from dawn to dusk, that was Kidlington. We were no longer members of society so we had no privileges. It was the system at its worst and it knocked the stuffing out of everyone who was sucked into it. That first night, I lay there thinking about my family, listening to the sobs from frightened kids all around me. It was grim. But I honestly didn't feel frightened. Somehow I knew this was my life now. I'd made my bloody bed and now I had to lie in it. I'd chosen this life and that's how it would be from now on. The system would try to crush me and all I could do was refuse to be destroyed. It wouldn't be easy.

We'd be up at 6am every day for a cold shower before

compulsory physical training come rain, snow or shine, and mostly it seemed to piss it down. We were marched everywhere military-style, slouching spines pushed straight, shoulders back, eyes forward. Anyone who fell out of line could expect a hard kick and a muttered oath. Most of the screws were ex-army and many had served in the war. They had fought Hitler to a standstill and thought we were a bunch of pansies by comparison with the Wehrmacht. Keeping us in line was easy money and they enjoyed the drill and discipline.

Despite this, on the whole, the guards were not cruel. They were not sadists like some of the men I met later in life inside the prison system, men who had become twisted and bent out of shape with bitterness and malice. They believed in making it tough for us to try to knock us into shape. To cure us of whatever social ills had seen us sent to Kidlington in the first place. They believed what they were doing was for the good of society.

Work six days a week was chopping lead until lunchtime, then we were marched back to the canteen, dozens of feet slapping the rough concrete floors in near-perfect time. A quick break over a plain lunch before another hour of PT then off to the workshop again until 5pm. It was hard and lonely and many of the younger lads cried themselves to sleep. There was no television, no radio, and we weren't even allowed to talk most of the time. We were always hungry, often tired, and every day was a process of surrender, losing another bit of our individuality to the system. It really was a short, sharp shock, and for many of us it succeeded. The only treat was writing one letter home a week. My spelling was poor and there was no one to ask for help because Billy and I were kept well apart. We used old-fashioned ink pens that dripped everywhere and my letters to Mum were a sight. She kept every one, though, and reading them after she died it struck me how quickly I had grown up in there.

If the letter writing was an outlet for our souls, physical

training was encouraged because it gave us an outlet for our aggression, of which there was plenty. I'd always kept in shape but I left feeling fitter than ever. I'd like to say I vowed never to go back inside but I can't. I knew I was risking my freedom to live beyond the law but it was a price I was prepared to pay. The night before my release I could hardly breathe. I was that excited about getting out.

When I was handed my bag of clothes it was like putting myself back on. My own underwear, my socks with holes, my trousers, crumpled shirt and hand-me-down jacket. I was stepping back into Micky Glückstad. As my train arrived back into Paddington station, it was another typical day in the capital. The city high-rises poked their snouts into the grey nothing. The rubbish that swirled along the train tracks was the only colour. It felt good to be home.

CHAPTER THREE

'CHAIRS WERE FLYING, BOTTLES SMASHING OVER GAMBLERS' HEADS AND THERE WAS BLOOD EVERYWHERE. I WATCHED OPEN-MOUTHED UNTIL THE POLICE ARRIVED AND THE BIG DANE, ROARING WITH LAUGHTER AT THE DESTRUCTION HE HAD UNLEASHED, HUSTLED ME OUT OF THE BACK DOOR BEFORE I GOT MY HEAD SMASHED OPEN...'

IF MY AUNT HAD BALLS, SHE'D BE MY UNCLE

It felt fantastic to be back home with my parents but my relief at being released didn't last long. Kidlington had changed me. I'd gone in a fresh-faced youngster and come out hardened. I was 16 and after three months' detention didn't care for anyone apart from my family. Any last softness had been well and truly beaten out of me by the regime behind bars. It had given me a fright but it had also taught me an important lesson – don't get caught. Otherwise, it's a mug's game. From now on it was Glückstad against the world.

Mum and Dad took my incarceration in their stride. They never nagged me, never told me I'd let them down. I was living at home with my parents but increasingly spending my time with an older bunch of lads. They guessed I was heading off the rails but struggled to stop me. No one could. I wasn't a bad kid, just in bad company and unable to walk away from the trouble that followed me wherever I went. My granddad Alfred knew the pressures of growing up in the East End. We'd stayed close since he taught me the rudiments of boxing and he always stuck up for me when I was in trouble with Mum and Dad.

'Leave the boy alone, Ivy. He's a good kid. It's not his fault if the other lads want to take him down a peg or two.'

But by now he was dead, having passed away aged 78 of pneumonia, thankfully before I got into real trouble with the law.

Even Granddad couldn't have stopped me slipping into the lifestyle that was to see me squander some of the best days of my life behind bars, make hundreds of thousands of pounds on the snide, own a Rolls-Royce and a Bentley – and blow the lot time and time again because it was easy come, easy go. It passed through my hands like water. I was a trouble magnet, pure and simple. I never looked for it but, sure as eggs are eggs, it came to me all the same. The early-morning knocks on the door became more frequent, and my scrapes with the law more serious. It was clearly only a matter of time before I came a major cropper and ended up incarcerated again.

In 1964 my family made one last effort to keep me out of prison, encouraging me to join the Norwegian merchant navy. In those days all you needed once you reached 16 was permission from your parents. So, in my smartest clothes, with my boots polished to a shine, I went to their headquarters at Lancaster Gate clutching the letter from Mum and a recommendation from Dad, who still had mates in the service. Within about six days I was a galley boy sailing for Belgium with a cargo of wheat from Royal Victoria Docks in Silvertown. My family waved me off at the docks and I felt a loneliness I'd never suffered even in the darkest days at Kidlington. It didn't last long. Within days I was scampering about the ship like a galley rat.

The crew of 60 or so were giants compared with me – hard-drinking, hard-womanising, hard-gambling, hard men from all over Europe, make no mistake. They all carried knives, and fights were the normal way of settling disputes. Many had missing fingers and horrific scars to prove it. It probably was to be the only honest job of my life. I was making good money – 30 quid a month with nothing to buy – and sending half home to Mum and Dad. If I'd got a job in London I would've been lucky to get two quid a week. And there was no work at home.

Following in my father's footsteps made me proud, and I was going to see the world beyond Plaistow. In the event, I spent most of my time at sea peeling potatoes under the dull galley lights and, when the seas were rough, throwing up into a bucket when I could reach it in time. On the plus side, I learned how to gamble and worked on my poker face. That was to be crucial when I became a professional conman and full-time wide boy.

Stopping in Antwerp to deliver our first cargo, I became friends with the Big Dane, as he was known. If the crew were giants he was their king, and everyone, even the captain, looked up to him as the below-decks leader. He dressed outrageously, at least for those days, in cowboy boots and a wide-brimmed Stetson hat, and must have stood six feet eight inches tall. He looked a mile wide, spoke in a booming voice, and I was scared to talk to him at first. Even his English was better than mine. But he took me under his wing for some reason and told everyone I was his little brother to keep me out of trouble.

I'd never seen a proper bar fight until my crewmates trashed a drinking den near the docks after the Big Dane fell out with some sailors from Somalia over a game of poker during a massive all-day drinking session. It was the Wild West all over again and made the East End look like a picnic. Chairs were flying, bottles smashing over gamblers' heads and there was blood everywhere. I watched open-mouthed until the police arrived and the Big Dane, roaring with laughter at the destruction he had unleashed, hustled me out of the back door before I got my head smashed open by one of the big wooden truncheons they carried.

Another time I fought the other galley rat, a lad about my age from Manchester called Jim who had been with the ship a year longer than me. I can't remember what we squabbled about but we were fighting Glasgow rules – butting, biting, punching and kicking each other while the off-duty crew cheered us on in the mess and took bets on the outcome. Neither one of us was prepared to back down or apologise, and we would have killed each other had the Big Dane not finally grabbed us both by the scruff of the neck and dangled us coughing and spluttering until we agreed to make up.

After Belgium, we sailed down the coast to France, then crossed the Atlantic to America. Howling gales and 70-mile-an-hour winds turned the ship into a giant rattle with us inside. The roar of the wind deadened even the relentless throb of the engines that echoed through the steel hull day and night, our constant companion. Hardened seamen gritted their teeth and made silent vows to St Brendan the Navigator, the patron saint of seafarers. Even the Big Dane, who laughed at his more superstitious cabin mates, shook his head and swore to me he'd never seen seas so high or rough. In the galley, pans of boiling water crashed to the floor and everything was wet, cold and stinking. For nearly the entire 12-day voyage we were tossed about like the crates of veg in the market back home. I thought it would never end but finally the winds died down and New York appeared suddenly out of the gloom of the Hudson River. Everything was clean and new and huge compared with Europe. The Statue of Liberty gleamed above us; skyscrapers towered over Manhattan.

For a working-class lad from Plaistow it was mind-blowing. London seemed very far away and very small. In the end, the Big Apple proved a disappointment. I was too young to drink legally and after Antwerp the crew wasn't taking any chances. Especially as the cops carried guns. I spent a couple of days wandering around the city on my own. The streets were wide and well swept, there were many more black people than I'd been used to at home and the cabs were yellow. I tried my charms on a few American girls but they just laughed at my accent. It was humiliating, so I didn't mind being back on board waiting for my shipmates.

From New York we steamed up to Canada, plying the trade route back and forth to Quebec via the Great Lakes until I had been on board for more than 10 months and considered myself as at home as anyone.

Finally, it was time to return and we made our way back into the Atlantic for our return journey to Tiger Bay in Wales. Three days out, we were warned over the radio that a major hurricane was forecast and the captain turned the ship back to Quebec. Everything that could move was tied down, portholes and bulkhead doors were secured and the crew lashed ropes to the decks and stairways to hold on to when it got really rough.

After our original crossing from England I couldn't imagine anything worse. But it got bad, quickly. The sky went black and the waves grew to 80 feet, slamming down over the ship and sending cranes, funnels and anyone stupid or unlucky enough to be in their path over the side, as 100-mile-an-hour winds blasted us. It felt like the end of the world had come. Everything was waterlogged and we were forced to bail bilge water in a bucket line from below decks as the electric pumps spluttered and struggled against the flood washing through the ship. After three or four days of sleepless hell the winds eased and our badly damaged ship limped back into Quebec. The cranes and funnels had gone and below decks was awash with water and vomit. We were stuck in port for a month while the ship was patched up. For my hardened shipmates, it was by far the closest most of them had come to death and they celebrated their survival with a colossal two-day bender.

We arrived in Wales a fortnight later after a smoother crossing. Cardiff was a rough old town in those days – it still is if you walk down the wrong street at the wrong time – and the docks were a regular rats' nest. My shipmates were thrilled to be on dry land again so they could continue their drinking and whoring. As soon as we'd unloaded our cargo, there was a stampede for shore leave led by the Big Dane, who tried to tempt me to go with him to a local brothel where he knew the madam.

But a year at sea was enough for me so I saw the captain and asked to be paid off. As I was leaving the empty ship with my duffel bag over my shoulder, I walked past the paymaster's cabin. The door was ajar and it was empty. The safe containing the ship's wages was open. I couldn't believe my good fortune and didn't hesitate. I slipped in and stuffed the bundles of notes into my sack before walking off the ship whistling. It was a fortune, thousands of pounds in cash, and I was shaking with fear that I'd be caught and beaten until I was safely on the train back to London. I never saw the Big Dane again but I heard later he'd been killed in a barroom brawl in Tangier when a coward stabbed him through the back and pierced his heart. He still managed to batter his killer unconscious before collapsing and dying in a pool of blood. He was a good man and taught me a lot.

Now I was back in London, running with my old gang and looking around as opportunities presented themselves. Given my recent haul I had no immediate need to work. I packed Mum and Dad off on holiday, telling them I'd had some lucky poker games, and sat back to decide what next. I had a growing reputation as a hard lad, someone who could take it as well as dishing it out, but, above all, could be trusted not to grass. I'd held back from getting involved in anything serious because going to prison was for mugs and, after Kidlington, I'd decided to try to watch my step a bit. Could things have turned out different for me? Of course they could. But there's no point speculating. As the old saying goes, 'if my aunt had balls, she'd be my uncle'.

Crime was taken seriously in the East End of old. There was a career ladder. You served your apprenticeship with a firm, specialising in whatever it was you were good at, then if you were lucky you graduated to running your own outfit. There were plenty of competing interests and some blokes freelanced, taking their skills where they were best rewarded. It could be highly lucrative for the talented but a nightmare if you didn't know what you were doing. There were 100 ways to graft a living below the radar, but 101 ways to get caught.

Those most admired by the wannabes like me were the safe-breakers. They were the master craftsmen of the criminal underworld. The security companies were always trying to come up with better ways of keeping them out. But the crackers, as they were known, stayed one step ahead. Gelignite, used in quarries and mines to break the rocks, was the first choice for safe-breaking. You filled the keyhole with jelly, lit the fuse and ran for cover. You had to be careful or you'd end up frying the contents, and more than one wannabe safe-cracker lost their fingers – and in a couple of cases their lives – messing with the explosives. Others found themselves blown across the room when the blast went off, shredded banknotes swirling into the air like confetti.

In the early days it was all about improvisation, learning just how much jelly was needed to crack the strongbox. I was never cut out to be a safe-breaker. My fingers were large and clumsy, more adept at swinging a punch than fiddling with a combination or trying to pick a lock with a hairpin. But I could work as a lookout and occasionally did, making sure I knew as little as possible about the job I was scouting for. It paid well and was relatively safe.

Next in the criminal hierarchy were the burglars. Often portrayed as the gentlemen of the underworld, they hunted in the so-called 'golden triangle' of Mayfair, Belgravia and Park Lane. Sometimes they would be tipped off by chauffeurs, butlers or other disgruntled staff. Some of the pros even used magazines like *Tatler* and *Country Life* to help pick their targets. The society diaries would be scoured like almanacs for events that could prove lucrative.

To the burglars, hard men like me were a lower form of life. Some of them thought we were parasites robbing those who couldn't afford it while they plundered the rich, sharing their spoils with the working classes – tipping waiters, tarts and doormen to redistribute the wealth. I knew a few decent porch-climbers who never got collared even once, but that wasn't my game either.

More to my liking were what we called jump-ups; they could be a very nice little earner if you were lucky and careful. We'd drive around until we saw a tasty-looking delivery lorry and follow it. When the driver stopped for a cup of tea, we'd leap in and drive off with his load. That's where the old saying 'it fell off the back of a lorry' originated. The goods would go to a middleman who'd fence them on the sly, sometimes to the very traders they had been destined for originally. Otherwise, we'd sell anything – food, car parts, toys, you name it. Booze was a favourite because it was easy to dispose of. You'd do the rounds of the pubs on a Friday night and make a few quid for the weekend selling the stash off cheaply.

Blaggers were the hardest and most feared men. They had most to lose, taking out security vans, banks and post offices armed with a shotgun, and prepared to use it. They had their own police unit, the Flying Squad, to contend with and faced long jail terms, rarely less than 10 years, if caught. I'd never fancied taking a life, nor losing my own to some trigger-happy copper in a pavement ambush, so steered well clear.

One of the Krays' big enterprises was the long firm fraud. It was simple and highly lucrative. A sham company would be set up at a warehouse premises and would start ordering goods. It didn't matter what they were, as long as they could be shifted on afterwards with no questions asked. The first few bills would be paid promptly, earning the confidence of the suppliers. After a few months, larger and more frequent orders would be made before the firm disappeared, leaving an empty warehouse and a string of unpaid bills behind it. It was easy money and felt like a victimless crime.

Using my noggin, I was starting to specialise in the con game, or cornering, as it was known colloquially. Billy Gibney had a nice ring. Christ only knows where he got it but it was worth something in the region of five grand. It was a chunky gold band with one massive diamond and two smaller ones on each side. It wasn't to my taste – it was the sort of bling you'd see these days on MTV – but it got the old grey matter going, and Billy, Arnie Fouste and myself cooked up a nice money-making scam.

First Arnie went to a jeweller he knew and had some Jekylls (Jekyll and Hyde – snide) made up. They looked the part but were strictly counterfeit and worth a fraction of Billy's. The diamonds were glass and the gold was a thin veneer over brass rather than the chunky original. An expert might have clocked them as fakes eventually, but to your man in the street they looked and felt like the real deal.

Next we motored up to Liverpool and booked into a hotel. Then we looked for a likely pub to do business in – somewhere a bit dodgy, where the governor might not mind a bit of illegitimate business on the premises, and might even fancy a shot at it himself. Arnie's job was to befriend the governor while I kept a low profile. Being Arnie, who we later nicknamed Arthur Daley after the wheeler-dealer *Minder* character, that would mean sitting at the bar talking to all and sundry until the boss dropped by to check on his customers and have a swift one himself before heading upstairs to his good lady wife. Arnie could talk the hind legs off a donkey and often did. Some drinks later, Arnie and the governor would be bezzie mates, buying each other rounds, telling each other stories and generally having a whale of a time. You couldn't help but like Arnie.

After a couple of days, Arnie would have a cash crisis and pull out Billy's ring as collateral for a loan of a hundred quid or so. Nothing major. At Arnie's urging, the pub boss would have it valued and you would see his eyes popping out when the jeweller told him it was worth £5,000. He loves the ring. Maybe thinks Arnie doesn't realise its true value. Next day, Arnie offers to sell it to him for £4,000. Well, the governor might like it but he hasn't got four grand lying about. OK, says Arnie, given that we're pals, it's yours for £2,500. The deal is agreed.

That's when I come in. The next day, as they're doing business, I walk in, tell Arnie he's a fucking crook and grab the ring.

'You owe me £600, you little scrote,' I snarl. 'I'm taking this ring as security unless you cough up now.'

Arnie looks worried sick as I stick the piece in my pocket and make to walk out. That's the beauty of the scam: now the landlord, who can see his 5-grand ring disappearing into the sunset, is doing Arnie a proper favour taking it off him.

'Now hang on a second, young man. Let's reach an agreement on this,' he says, and we're in business. He gives Arnie the cash, Arnie hands over £600 to me and I give the guv'nor the ring, after I've palmed it in my pocket for one of the snides. Everyone's happy. At least until the new owner finally gets it valued.

It was the perfect swindle, near enough. No violence, no police and no nastiness. After splitting the money, we bombed it back down to London, laughing all the way. We must have done this scam a dozen times around the country over the years and never once got a tug.

I prided myself on being a criminal's conman. I didn't rip off ordinary Joes. Most of the people we took on this were villains themselves in some way or another who'd made a pile of dosh and invested it in a boozer or a hotel. They certainly weren't everyday folks. Let's face it, anyone who has got two grand plus, a very tidy sum in those days, to blow on a ring from some geezer they've only just met is unlikely to get the law involved and risk looking like a mug.

CHAPTER FOUR

'DRAGGED TO THE PUNISHMENT BLOCK IN A DAZE, I FELT A SHARP JAB IN MY BUM AND EVERYTHING WENT BLACK. THE NEXT DAY I CAME TO IN A STRAITJACKET. MY FACE WAS SWOLLEN AND MY LIPS WERE CRACKED. DRIED BLOOD FLAKED OFF MY FACE...'

BORSTAL BOY

The barrel of the sawn-off shotgun prodded me in the chest. It was so close I could smell a mix of gun oil and the stale sweat of its owner. Looking down the business end of a deadly weapon was a sobering experience, not exactly how we'd planned our Friday night. But Jack 'The Hat' McVitie, the proud owner of the shooter that was jabbing me in the sternum, didn't give a fuck. He was like a wild man: red-faced, shaking and sweating, with spit dribbling down his chin. And he was waving his gun round the crowded bar like a lunatic. If it went off, there would be a massacre and the unfortunate cleaners would be picking bits of customers out of the plush red drapes for weeks to come.

In the late sixties the Regency Club in Hackney was the place to be seen. Ronnie and Reggie Kray had a share in the bar and their underworld glamour attracted a young, hip crowd who fancied themselves rotten. I didn't give a toss about the punters or their showing off, but it was a decent enough place for a quiet drink, especially if you knew the guv'nors.

Billy Gibney and I had dropped in to try to pick up some work from the Twins. The barman told us we'd missed them.

What the hell; we decided to stay and have a drink anyway. So there we were, propping up the bar, having a tipple with Arnie Fouste, minding our own business and not looking for trouble. Suddenly, there was a commotion at the door and a woman screamed as a well-known, much-feared local villain, Jack 'The Hat' McVitie, stormed into the bar armed with a nasty-looking sawn-off. McVitie was a notorious so and so – an enforcer, hitman and brawler. He lived for trouble, didn't give a damn for the consequences and was clearly off his tits on booze and pills. He was looking for the Krays – and not for a friendly chinwag either.

The full story emerged later. McVitie had been offered cash-for-corpses work by the Twins but had bottled it and cheated them out of their money. Obviously this was a big no-no with Ron and Reg. But Jack was Jack so they gave him a second chance. To put things straight, and prove his loyalty, Ron ordered him to shoot a former business associate, Leslie 'The Brain' Payne. The Brain had helped the Twins build the Firm, turning them from the original East End hard men into businessmen. More than anyone, perhaps, he had set them on the road to moneyed respectability and the entry it allowed into posh society. But they had fallen out and feared he was going to grass on them – a crime punishable by death in the East End.

McVitie – a small and vain man, called 'The Hat' because he habitually wore a trilby to hide the fact that he was losing his hair – was given a gun and advanced £300, with another £300 to follow on completion of the hit. The silly sod took the money but never did the job. Who knows if he had a death wish, but he spared Payne. Legend has it he knocked at his door and was told by Payne's fast-thinking missus that his victim-to-be was out. McVitie left, Payne survived and the erstwhile hitman never repaid the Krays' money. From then on, it was only a matter of time before he came a proper cropper. No one made Ron and Reg look like mugs.

Now here he was drunk and spoiling for trouble in the

Regency, while half of East London was trying to have a quiet drink and a natter. It was tense as fuck. Not the way the night was supposed to turn out. McVitie was ranting and raving, demanding to see Reg and Ron.

'Where are those c**ts?' he muttered. 'I need to see them now.'

I might have been 19 and the youngest person there but I'd never been one to panic. I was a big lump for my age. Five foot ten and muscular after Kidlington and a year at sea, and I could handle myself. People have said I have no fear because I look at life differently from normal people. You're alive and then you're dead. And you don't usually get a choice which one. So why worry? This was the first time I'd been on the wrong end of a shooter, though, and we were sweating.

I remember it like it was yesterday.

McVitie is plastered and properly out of control. Leaning back towards the bar, I reach behind me and casually wrap my fingers around the neck of a champagne bottle. This mad slag ain't going to take my life for no reason, I think. If I am going to drop McVitie, I'll have to finish him or he'll spend the rest of his life trying to kill me. For several moments I'm thinking, I've got a front-row ticket to a massacre. Luckily for both of us, Arnie is calm and encourages McVitie to put down his gun and have a drink. Slowly, he comes back down to earth, all the time Arnie talking quietly to him, convincing him that shooting up Reg and Ron's favourite club isn't a great move. He'll get nicked before he's out of the door and a bent copper will finish the job in prison for the Twins. The whole incident lasts only two or three minutes before McVitie stalks out – the cops aren't even called – but it feels like an hour and the back of my shirt and jacket are soaked through with sweat. Even today, I get the shivers thinking about that gun pointing in my face.

It didn't end well for McVitie. A few months later, in October 1967, he was lured to a flat in Stoke Newington on the pretext of a party. According to legend, Reg Kray put a gun against his head and pulled the trigger. The gun failed to fire so the brothers stabbed McVitie repeatedly with a carving knife they'd found in the flat. It was a bloodbath. Reg, who nicked his hand during the killing, was asked afterwards how he'd injured himself. He reputedly replied: 'Gardening.'

McVitie's body was never found. Depending on who tells the story, he was either dumped overboard from a boat at Newhaven with a lump of concrete for company, buried in an unmarked grave in a South London cemetery, chopped up and fed to pigs, or buried in the foundations of the Bow Flyover. I fancy the latter. Think of that next time you're driving down the A12 past the London 2012 Olympics site. That was how lives ended back in the day. You lived fast but ended up in concrete if you were too fast, or not fast enough. Dying young was practically a contractual obligation. Whatever happened, it was thanks to him, in part at least, that I ended up in borstal – which is where I was when he met his end.

Our close shave had made us thirsty and Billy suggested we drive to Soho for last orders. There was a cellar bar, the Alphabet Club, in Gerrard Street, that was good for a drink and a laugh after hours. Popular with the ladies, too, who were good for a kiss and cuddle round the back if you were favoured. We picked up our pal Stevie Sawyer on the way. Arriving in Soho, I dropped the boys outside the club then left my Ford Zodiac six-pot parked up round the corner in Wardour Street.

By the time I got to the Alphabet, it was chaos. Stevie was sitting on his arse at the bottom of the stairs, blood pouring from his nose and down his shirt. Billy was pinned against a wall by a huge doorman. I was at the top of the stairs, just about to go down. Not knowing I was with them, the doorman turned to me and shouted: 'Fuck off, prick, we're full up.'

That was all I needed. After having a gun shoved in my face, I was wound tighter than a rope and raging fit to burst. His attention was focused on Billy. His big pink hands were wrapped around Bill's neck and my mate's face was rapidly turning blue. I bent down to pick up a brick from the gutter, then thought better of it: 'No, I can take this slag on my own.'

Jumping down the stairs two at a time into the grimy basement, I steamed in, punching the big bouncer in the head. He dropped Bill and came at me panting like a fucking Rottweiler and with breath to match. I stepped back and kicked at his knee to distract him, then punched him in the head. Bang. Bang. Bang. As he sank to his knees, I booted him in the kidneys. He'd be pissing blood for weeks. He hit the floor like a sack of spuds, hollering fit to wake the dead, but nobody came to help him. Pulling Stevie and Billy from the floor and back up the stairs, we ran for it. The bouncer's professional pride was firmly on the floor along with his front teeth. Spitting blood, he shouted after us: 'Don't come back, you c**ts.'

We legged it back to the car, laughing like maniacs. I covered the plates in case we'd been followed. Billy went to get in the driver's seat. He was the fastest behind the wheel, but I warned him: 'Sure, Bill, but not too quick.'

I knew we'd attract attention if we went hell for leather through the quiet streets. Sure enough, as we were leaving Soho, a police Wolseley 6/90 pulled up behind us, its bell ringing. An evil coincidence or someone had clocked us and called the Old Bill. We didn't stick around to find out. As the copper got out of his car, Bill floored the accelerator and we shot forward in a cloud of exhaust smoke and screeching tyres, leaving the officer scrambling back into his car looking a right fanny. Setting a furious pace, Billy took us roaring through the backstreets of central London, losing the copper easily in the warren of junctions between Tottenham Court Road and Holborn. Bill really knew how to throw a car about. If he'd become a racing driver, he'd have been someone today, a regular Lewis Hamilton at the very least.

If only we'd called it a night then. If you ask me, the road to hell ain't paved with good intentions, it's paved with 'if onlys'. But I felt we deserved a drink after our dust-up. Stevie shot off so Bill and I headed to a little drinking club in Forest Gate, and enjoyed some hospitality. In all honesty, we were probably knocking it back at a fair old pace. And alcohol and trouble go hand in hand in my book.

But it didn't kick off until Billy and I were leaving. Three passing coppers pegged me as a local troublemaker – in those days the police knew everyone on their patch – and stopped us for a bit of fun. Billy was dressed rather loudly, to put it mildly. Swirled patterns, gingham shirts and wide trousers were all the rage at the time. The cops didn't like the look of Billy or me.

In fact, the feeling was mutual. But they had a police Alsatian dog with them. And Billy liked dogs even less than he liked the Old Bill. Seeing his discomfort, the copper holding the snarling beast let it strain right up against its leash, into our nuts, and laughed: 'You're not so flash now, are you?'

Cops can smell trouble and we must have reeked of it after our night out. 'Where you been, lads?' one of them asked.

I was feeling indestructible after our bust-up and the booze, and told them where they could go. These days the police are nice as pie and as politically correct as anyone. Not back then. It was truncheons out and questions later at the first sign of trouble. Before we could argue, we were up against a wall with the snarling police dog tearing at its lead in its efforts to savage us.

'What's in the car then?' asked the first copper.

'I'll stay here and stop this one running away and you take Glückstad here and search it.'

They were looking for drugs or weapons but I knew the car was clean. I prided myself on that little motor and wasn't so stupid as to carry anything incriminating on an ordinary night out. So my heart sank when one of the coppers proudly brandished a bag of coloured speed pills – bombers they called them back then – and asked what it was. It was an old-school fit-up. I was being done good and proper. All three of them started to laugh. And that was that. I wasn't taking that kind of grief after the night we'd had. Out of the corner of my eye I saw Billy tensing up for trouble and let the adrenalin rush take over. Without batting an eyelid, I booted the dog in the ribs, leaving it yelping on the pavement, following with a flurry of kicks before it could tear my knackers off. The dog handler hit me across the back with his truncheon so I turned and belted him in the face. It was a great punch, breaking his nose and doubling him up in agony. One nil. I knuckled another copper in the back and he fell to the floor, yelling for help, but before we could run for it someone blew their whistle and more police arrived. They must have been waiting round the corner. It was a proper dust-up. And they gave us a real good hiding.

In court the next day with two black eyes I must have looked like a giant panda. But a trip to the zoo wasn't in the offing. It was somewhere much worse for carrying drugs and fighting the coppers, no matter how much provocation. Because I was 19 and had already done youth detention, I was sent to borstal. Billy got six months' detention, and the police dog had to be put down.

I was taken straight to Wormwood Scrubs prison in West London before I could be allocated a borstal. Walking through the gates with the other new arrivals, we caught a glimpse of the exercise yard and I spotted Bill Curbishley and Harry Roberts walking together. Roberts was doing three life sentences as Britain's most notorious cop killer with a recommendation he serve 30 years before being eligible for parole. He's still inside to this day.

Curbishley had been nicked with Roy Shaw for armed robbery of a security van in Longfield, Kent, even though he and Shaw had never met. Another fit-up par excellence by Her Majesty's forces of law and order. But looking at that pair put my troubles in perspective. I thought I had problems but at least I could see the end of my sentence without a long-range telescope. After six weeks of relative peace and quiet, keeping my head firmly down for once, I was shipped off to Rochester borstal.

As the prison bus took us out of London and into the Kent countryside, I realised I hadn't been out of the Smoke for years. The fields and orchards looked like Norway but Rochester was grim. It had started raining hard as we crossed the River Medway on the big iron road bridge. A thick fog had come down, shrouding the town in a ghostly murkiness, and the borstal loomed large and menacing ahead of us. As the sweatbox carrying me and five other cons pulled up, our driver tooted his horn and the big black gates swung open. Rochester was an old institution even then; evil and forbidding like something out of Dickens, which I suppose it was in a way. That was handy because the great writer had lived nearby when he was already world famous. Originally known as Borstal prison, Rochester had been the first ever reformatory for young offenders. And because of that the name became synonymous with other detention centres for troubled young men across the country.

Borstal training, as it was known, was designed to knock even the most hardened young thugs into shape and turn out productive, or at least not destructive, members of society. Some hope. Because Rochester was the original borstal, the screws took a perverse pride in being the hardest and most brutal. Good or bad, they treated us all like the right little toerags we were and the poisonous atmosphere infected everyone. You could almost smell the testosterone-fuelled aggression of several hundred young men locked up in close proximity to one another. It dripped from the ceilings and swirled round the site, thick and evil like the fog on the River Medway. It was no place for a wilting flower – the cons and the screws bullied weaker inmates remorselessly – and I had no intention of being one.

Within a few days I'd marked my territory and it was known

inside that I was someone not to be messed with. I didn't go looking for trouble but, if it found me, I didn't exactly shy away either. To show weakness was an error you'd end up paying for over and over again. But I couldn't abide bullies either, be they screws or cons. So, if I saw someone trying it on with one of the weaker inmates, I'd more often than not step in and sort things out. That was just the way I was. Fair was fair, even behind 15-foot walls and barbed wire. I didn't fancy myself as the prison 'daddy' but I wasn't anyone's mug either. I kept my distance and a sharp lookout for the opportunity to get the hell out.

I had been allocated to A Wing. It had three wings, each with three dormitories, 16 borstal boys to a dorm. Facing the house was B Wing, containing another 48 or so lads, some shipped in from Feltham, where there had been riots, and others from Dover, the result of similar internal bust-ups. All the toughest cases under one roof. It was a recipe for disaster and the pot had been bubbling dangerously for weeks already when I arrived.

A couple of months or so later, all us from A Wing were marching past the B Wing dorm on the way to the gym for another PT session when the alarm went off and the screws rushed in mob-handed and truncheons at the ready to stamp on the trouble before it got out of control.

I was never one to miss a chance and, frankly, after a month of borstal they could stick their correctional facility up their collective arses. Up at the crack of dawn for physical training, rubbish food and long hours of manual labour outside the walls, I was done with it and to hell with the consequences.

I took a chance and slipped away from the gym party, heading towards the wall as fast as my legs could carry me. There was no plan B, but with the chaos enveloping the jail I thought I had a fair to medium chance of making it over and away. But my escape fell apart sooner than I expected when three screws from the prison reception spotted me. 'Glückstad, what the hell are you doing? Get back here now,' one shouted as they barrelled towards me in full riot gear.

Something inside me snapped. I was sick of being shouted at. Looking around for something to defend myself with, I spotted a ropey-looking wall. Giving it a good hoof with my prison-issue boots, I broke off half a crumbling brick and hurled it at my pursuers. As luck would have it, it caught the first screw, a particularly vicious bugger who delighted in tormenting his charges for no good reason, on the side of the head and he went down blotto, lights out. Hole in one! But there was no time to celebrate. The other two were on me in seconds, kicking and punching me and giving me a good working over with their truncheons. I gave as good as I got until one of them got his arm round my neck from behind and squeezed until I passed out. Forget Goodnight Vienna, it was Goodnight Glückstad.

Dragged to the punishment block in a daze, I felt a sharp jab in my bum and everything went black. The next day I came to in a straitjacket. My face was swollen and my lips were cracked. Dried blood flaked off my face. They kept me there for two days without food or water. Not a drop. When a visiting magistrate finally arrived to clear up the mess, I was shipped off to Reading borstal to be welcomed with 28 days' bread and water, and another beating as punishment for trying to escape and knocking out a screw. In principle, borstals were designed to be educational rather than punitive and to have a focus on discipline and routine. Officially, the only corporal punishment was the birch for mutiny or assaulting an officer. This could be ordered only by the visiting magistrates, subject in each case to the personal approval of the Home Secretary. In practice, the screws knew they had to maintain order, and maintain it they did. I'm not claiming they were all hard nuts or bullies. But there were enough of those to make life very tough for anyone who stepped out of line. We were banned from talking while working, so you learned to mutter to your neighbour out of the corner of your mouth. It's been said that's why so many ex-lags mumble, as you got so used to speaking like that to avoid the screws' attentions.

My reputation from Rochester had preceded me and there was no messing around when I arrived. The screws were practically waiting on the doorstep with truncheons drawn. They beat the fuck out of me, working over my arms, legs and body as I fought for my life, kicking and punching until they overwhelmed me by sheer force of numbers. Dragged to a padded cell where the stink of piss and dried blood was intolerable, I was left in a pile, coughing my guts up and groaning in agony.

The next day, black and blue, I was up before another visiting magistrate and sentenced to three months extra inside for fighting, then allocated to the prison's wood shop. For a short period I kept my nose clean and stayed out of trouble. The ferocity of that beating had shaken my confidence. It wouldn't stay shaken for very long. Reading was a very tough prison for properly out-of-control borstal boys. And I just couldn't stay out of trouble. For some reason, this infuriated the screws and they baited me at every opportunity. As a result, I spent Christmas on bread and water and saw in the New Year of 1968 in solitary confinement.

But I wasn't going to let them beat me. Every time they sent me into chokey (as we called solitary) I came smiling back for more – I was like Steve McQueen in *The Great Escape*, the original 'Cooler King'. I knew I couldn't let them break me. And I didn't. Screws might be a pretty unimaginative bunch but even they get bored eventually when they fail to break a man. After three months, they couldn't wait to be rid of me and I was off to borstal on the Isle of Portland in Dorset. It took only the hardest cases from all over the country. I don't know who was more relieved – them, I hope.

Handcuffed between two guards, I arrived at Portland to find that, once again, my reputation as a hard, uncompromising man had preceded me. Portland was OK as far as I was concerned. I had my own cell for the first time and the food was good by prison standards. But I was ripe to be taken down a peg or two. And it didn't take long before I had my first fight. This time it was the inmates looking to score points against Micky G. Johnny Seagers was a Hackney boy and hard as concrete, a big bastard and no mistake. Six feet of solid muscle and a fitness fanatic to boot, always doing push-ups in his cell. Before being nicked for armed robbery on a security van, he'd sparred with the legendary Henry Cooper and had a tasty left hook. Inside, no one had ever beaten him and he was the closest there was to a 'King of the Borstals'. He was the governor of Portland in all but name and didn't like the thought of a pretender to his crown. The pressure between us built up until there was only one way it was going to be settled.

Portland was in a God-awful spot. The prison looked like a row of rotting teeth against the skyline when we were outside on work details. It wasn't much better inside so everyone tried to get out as much as they could, even if it involved shovelling shit all day as it normally did. There was only one road on and off the island and escape wasn't a serious option, so trustees, not guards, supervised the work parties on the whole. The authorities must have been making money hand over fist hiring us out to the local yokels. It was back-breaking work, and normally so cold your hands and feet would freeze. More than a couple of the lads lost a toe or two to a clumsy spade and never felt it, as their feet were so numb.

The pressure between Seagers and me had been building for weeks so it was no surprise when he finally faced me down one grim afternoon under a skull-grey sky while we were on farm detail bagging up manure. Sensing trouble, the main form of entertainment for long-timers, a group of cons had gathered to watch the big man give me a pounding with his weapon of choice, his fists. Afterwards, as usual, no one would have seen a thing.

I could smell stale sweat and cigarettes as Seagers towered

over me, fists balled at his sides, expecting me to back down and grovel for mercy. I expected a beating, but there was no point waiting. Maybe that's hard to understand. But the hard man will never back down even when he's out-gunned, outnumbered and out of luck. Throwing down my shovel, I snarled, 'Come on then, you slag,' tucked my head in and threw myself at him, fists swinging in a flurry of tight punches.

He was a tough man to knock down, and boxed well. We circled each other like animals, each looking for a weak spot to exploit. Seagers had some game in him. I was puffing like a steam train in the cold winter air and took a couple of blows to the head as we danced around jabbing, testing each other out ahead of a killer blow. We sparred for 10 minutes before I thought, Fuck this, and threw myself at Seagers. Pushing him back, as his feet scrabbled in the mud for purchase, I gave him an uppercut to the jaw followed by two or three rib-breakers. I'm sure I heard a crack and he yelled in pain as the wind rushed out of his lungs like a popped balloon. I was out of steam, but so was Seagers. We were hitting each other like a pair of girls. Then he grabbed me by the arms, as if to crush me. Suddenly I felt a sharp pain in my right ear. Seagers had bitten the top off it and warm blood was pouring down the side of my face. I lunged upwards, smashing the top of my head into his jaw, and he went down in the mud, shattered. Gasping for breath, we were pulled apart, bloody and covered in shit.

Despite the ear-biting incident – 30 years ahead of Mike Tyson – it had been an evenly matched contest. That's fighting for you. It ain't fair and there are no rules. I'd have ripped off both of Seagers' ears and his nose for good luck if I'd had the chance. I wasn't afraid to admit that. Pride had been maintained on both sides. Back inside, my bloodied and muddied appearance was noted by one of the screws and I was hauled in front of the governor. He was a war veteran with a wooden leg and even I knew he wouldn't stand for any nonsense.

'Glückstad, what happened to your ear?' he asked.

'I was working on an outside party, sir,' I told him straight-faced. 'There was a horse nearby and I went up to stroke it and the bloody thing bit my ear off, sir.'

'That is funny, Glückstad,' replied the governor, equally straight-faced. 'We had Seagers in here earlier and that same horse broke three ribs when it kicked him.'

'Some strange things happen in prison, sir.'

'Well, I can't nick the horse so no further action will be taken. That's all, Glückstad.'

'Thank you, sir.'

I'm sure I saw a gleam in the old devil's eye as I was marched out of his office by the screws. From that day on, there was a grudging respect between myself and Seagers and, when the cops later put pressure on him to finger me as part of his blagging gang, he refused. The governor had the last laugh, though. After that he put me on kitchen detail, carting dustbins full of slops into the prison gardens every morning. It was exhausting, spreading the slops on the allotments where inmates grew carrots and potatoes, but I enjoyed it. In the afternoons they had me scrubbing floors, miles of them. When I was finished with one landing, they'd make me do it all over again. It was repetitive and back-breaking but it didn't bother me. I let my mind wander back to the East End, daydreaming about my family and friends, and the remaining months passed easily.

CHAPTER FIVE

'I LOOKED OVER AT DANNY AND PAUL AND LAUGHED. THE BLOOD WAS RUNNING FAST IN MY VEINS AND I FELT STRONG, CONFIDENT AND AGGRESSIVE. THERE WAS NOTHING I LIKED BETTER THAN TO GIVE A BULLY THEIR COMEUPPANCE. FIGHTING IN FRONT OF THE KRAYS WAS AN HONOUR TOO. I KNEW I'D GIVE A GOOD ACCOUNT OF MYSELF WHATEVER HAPPENED...'

ON THE ROAD WITH THE GYPSIES

Touring traveller sites for bare-knuckle bouts was lucrative but hard graft. There are some very tough gypsy fighters who revel in their ability to soak up punishment. In the movie *Snatch*, Brad Pitt's character 'One Punch' Mickey O'Neil is a fair representation of some of the travellers I'd been fighting for money since my late teens. They were tough, wiry little bastards who didn't know when they were beaten. For my part, I suffered one or two right kickings in my time and I'm not ashamed to admit that a couple of them came from very handy gypsy fighters.

The rules were simple: as many three-minute rounds as it took until one man was on his arse and couldn't fight any more. The gypsies didn't like submissions as a rule. Anyone who gave up in the ring risked a kicking afterwards, depending on how heavily he'd been backed. Fights took place in a marked-out ring, or sometimes on a wooden platform, surrounded by boozed-up travellers baying for blood. I fought a heady mix of novice fighters, wannabes trying to prove themselves, and grizzled old hacks with a bit of experience and some technique. But the money was good, sometimes as much as 400 or 500 quid a fight, with more to be earned if you had someone putting money on you outside the ring.

I enjoyed spending time with gypsies. They were generally decent folk and, with my Norwegian roots, I felt I had a lot in common with them as an outsider.

On one occasion I was having a quiet drink with my mates Dave Carr and Roy Neal on the way back from a job in the Midlands. Dave had been playing pool with some gypsies in the back of the pub and was getting quite animated. When he came over with a pint in his hand, I saw the gleam in his eye and a grin on his lips and knew something was about to go down.

'Micky,' he confessed, 'I've arranged for you to have a bare-knuckle fight with one of the gypsies. There's quite a group gathering and they're keen as mustard. It'll be no bother for a man of your talents.'

I wasn't keen but I looked over at the group and they didn't look so big from where I was standing. In all honesty, I still wasn't that enthusiastic. I hadn't come out to fight, but Dave continued: 'I've wagered a grand on you – if you win we'll split it 50–50. How does that sound?'

'Done.'

The gypsies were living in a car park at the back of the pub. There were about 20 caravans and quite a crowd had gathered as I stepped outside with Roy and Dave, stripping off my shirt and flexing my arms and neck to warm up. There was a little chap dancing around and joking with the travellers. I thought he was the fighter and laughed inwardly. This would be no trouble at all – easy money like Dave had promised.

Then someone shouted and one of the blokes banged on the door of a nearby caravan. Out stepped a giant of a man. He must've been six foot five and 18 stone of pure muscle, built like a battle tank. This was their champion. I looked over at Dave and shook my head. He couldn't believe it either. We'd been done good and proper by the gypsies. There was nothing for it; I'd have to fight this man mountain.

The gypsies made a ring and we faced each other down. My opponent was bald and grizzled with a real snarl on his lips. He stretched out a couple of times then nodded to the referee. He'd not said a word to me.

One of the gypsies bashed a bucket and it was fight on. The big bloke lumbered towards me and I saw my opportunity. He was huge but he was slow. I could take him if I moved fast. I feinted a blow to his head with my right then jabbed at his ribs with my left, catching him very hard two or three times. He gasped and before he could bring his arms down to protect his body I followed with a fearful right to his ribs. There was a terrific crack and he folded, the wind knocked out of him. But before I could follow it up he was back at me, recovering quickly and throwing some breezy punches in the direction of my head. I darted back, jogging from foot to foot and looking for an opportunity. It didn't take long; despite his size, he had no technique and left himself wide open.

Without warning I threw a roundhouse to the side of his head and caught him a glancing blow over the right eye. As he ducked away I came up under his guard with an uppercut and he was seeing stars. He lumbered towards me but the fight had gone out of him and I could see his legs and arms were jelly. I jabbed a couple of times – his arms were flailing in front of him – then, sensing an opening, I landed a full-on right hook to his jaw. He was down and out. The gypsies were going wild. They loved a good ruck, even when their own man was getting leathered, and we'd given them one.

Dave picked up our winnings and we were back inside for a last drink before motoring back to London. Winning felt good.

In between fights, I met one of the underworld legends of that era. I first saw Frank Mitchell, who was known as 'The Mad Axeman', when I was visiting a pal of mine in Dartmoor prison where he was doing five years for grievous bodily harm. Mitchell was in the visiting hall and my mate said he was nice as pie inside, and even bred budgerigars, despite his alarming nickname. He was a big bloke, over six feet tall and at least 16 stone, but he didn't have much upstairs and kept getting caught. His party trick was to lift two of the biggest blokes in the room off the ground, one on each arm, and he was a fanatical bodybuilder.

Ronnie Kray had befriended Mitchell while they were serving time together in Wandsworth prison. He thought Mitchell had been given a raw deal by the authorities, who were refusing to give him a release date. So the Krays masterminded a plan to spring him from Dartmoor so he could work for them. The rumour was that they had someone they wanted him to kill. On 12 December 1966, he escaped after being allowed as a trusted prisoner to take a walk on the moors. The Krays' men were waiting for him and whisked him back to London.

The next time I saw Mitchell was at a flat the Twins had hired for him to hide out in on Barking Road, East Ham. I'd been sent by Roy Neal to sort out the keys. Mitchell claimed he remembered me but he wasn't in good shape and I didn't know whether I believed him or not. He was already bored out of his mind from being cooped up and it was obvious he was mentally ill. Within days of his escape, he'd risked his freedom – and that of his rescuers – by sending scrawled letters to *The Times* and *Daily Mirror* asking the Home Secretary for a pardon.

The Krays simply couldn't afford to have Mitchell going native on them. They had too much to lose. On Christmas Eve, a van pulled up outside the flat and the unsuspecting Axeman got in. He was never seen alive again and his body was never found. Some claim he was dumped at sea, a favourite among East End villains at the time. I know for a fact he was shot dead because he was uncontrollable and the Krays were worried he would take them back to prison with him.

It was a sad end to a big man with a bigger reputation and a reminder that life can be 'nasty, brutish and short'. But no one was going to bring it up when I next saw the Krays out and about.

Sometime later, I was with Danny Woollard and another old and trusted pal called Paul at Barnet Horse Fair. Paul was trying to sell a horse so Danny and I went along for the ride. The annual September shindig in Barnet is famous among the travelling community and attracts a fair few bare-knuckle fighters behind the scenes. In recent years, the event's cleaned up its act, made itself a bit more family friendly, but back in the day it was a weekend's worth of bashed heads, heavy drinking and illegal gambling – a great day out in my book for sure!

That day we couldn't get a buyer for Paul's horse so we tied it up to a beer tent and went inside for a drink. Who should be in the bar but the Kray Twins and Donny 'The Bull' Adams, a hard-faced bloke, about six feet tall, who fancied himself the best fighter in England and was known for a while as King of the Gypsies for his prowess in the ring. Horse fairs were his bread and butter; he would travel across the country and fight where he could find an opponent. Today there was no one to take him on so he was slowly getting hammered with the Twins.

As usual Ron and Reg were immaculately turned out. They looked more like stockbrokers than faces, especially surrounded by gypsies. But Ron and Reg always respected the travelling community and, in return, were valued as straight talkers who wouldn't cause any trouble. For their part, they loved watching the bare-knuckle bouts as much as anyone and would bet heavily.

We were having a drink and a chinwag about old times when Paul's horse decided it wasn't getting enough attention and stuck its head through a gap in the canvas, nuzzling Ronnie's arm and leaving a mark on his suit. We all laughed – Ronnie had taken it in good humour – but Adams, who appeared to have been drinking heavily and hadn't contributed much to the conversation, mumbled, 'Fucking horse,' and smacked the animal right on the nose. It reared up in fright and pulled part of the tent over as it collapsed in a heap. Paul and Danny rushed out and pulled it to its feet. The Krays were silent but Adams was laughing fit to burst and I could feel my blood rising at his sucker punch and general attitude. Looking Adams in the eye, I asked him: 'Would you like to try and hit me like that?'

Adams looked me up and down. I hadn't met him before but Danny, who had previously had a number of run-ins with The Bull, told me he might be big but he was a coward who wouldn't take on a real man.

'Put on four stone then come back and see me,' he laughed. 'In any case, I only fight for money, and you three don't look as if you have any.'

'Me, Danny or Paul will fight you,' I replied. 'Take your pick. If you win you can have the horse – it's worth at least £500. If you lose, you give us £500.'

As I was smaller than Paul and Danny, and didn't have a reputation then, I could see Adams thinking I would be easy meat. In fact, that's what I had been counting on.

Within minutes we were outside and surrounded by a circle of 40 or 50 gypsies. Danny asked Ron Kray: 'Ron, will you make sure this fight's straight up?'

Without a pause he replied: 'Don't worry, lads, you'll get fair play.'

Adams had plenty of gypsy mates with him but I reckoned they would be more than happy for me to give him a good hiding. And, with Ron's guarantee, no one was going to dive in mob-handed. It would be just how I liked it, one on one.

Danny was my second and Adams, who must've weighed 16 stone to my 12, had another old hand, Tommy 'The Bear' Brown, who was his trainer and mentor, as his number two. I took off my shirt and stretched, my Jesus tattoo getting a fair bit of attention from the gypsies, swinging my arms to get the blood moving. Adams had also stripped to the waist, showing off a muscular torso, but one that had clearly seen better days.

'Make ready,' shouted the referee, another gypsy fella.

I looked over at Danny and Paul and laughed. The blood was running fast in my veins and I felt strong, confident and aggressive. There was nothing I liked better than to give a bully their comeuppance. Fighting in front of the Krays was an honour too. I knew I'd give a good account of myself whatever happened. Across the circle, I could see Adams mouthing obscenities at me.

A lot of blokes will try to psych you out before a single punch has been thrown. It's called sledging in gentlemen's sports such as cricket. On the cobbles, I call it being a c**t. But it's never bothered me unduly. Let the silly sods work themselves into a right old frenzy. More often than not, it's a sign they've no bottle anyway. Cool and calm heads usually win the day. So I ignored the abuse, concentrating instead on staring deep into the ugly fucker's eyes, and imagined planting my fist squarely between them. That would give the cock something to swear about.

With a bang on an upturned bucket, we were off. 'Make your Mum proud,' I hissed through my teeth as Donny came at me.

Adams tried, as many big men did, to overwhelm me in the first few seconds by sheer size and body weight. His arms were flailing and I realised his technique was poor to non-existent. I met him halfway and we were trading heavy blows back and forward but I wasn't moving even when he was hitting me with his best punches. He was hard and my body blows were making little impact. But every time I hit his head it jarred him.

The tinkers were screaming fit to wake the dead.

'Do him. Kill him.' It was like the Coliseum in Rome. I wasn't sure who they were screaming for but I suspected it wasn't me.

I could see Danny and Paul jumping about like crazy outside the ring as I circled Adams, looking for a way past his fists to his face. Then I roared like a lion and sent a sharp right flying into the side of his head. He howled and staggered away, fending off my punches to his head with his elbows in a typical fighter's crouch. Not so clever now, laughing boy, I thought.

After about 10 minutes, we were both dripping with sweat and I could see Adams tiring. Clearly, he didn't know what to do with me. Despite a size difference that would have cancelled out any chance of us meeting in a professional ring, I'd soaked up everything he had thrown at me and kept him on the back foot. He stepped backwards and sunk down on to one knee, exhausted. As he struggled to get up, a swift knee to the knackers lessened the chances of him bringing any more wankers into the world. The crowd flinched as Donny fell back on to his arse, finished. He made a final attempt to get up but I swatted him with a last blow to the head and he went down spark out to a massive roar of approval. By now, as word had gone round there was a fight on the cards, the crowd had grown to several hundred, and no one could believe I'd floored Donny. But the evidence was there in front of them, coughing and puking, awake after one of his mates had thrown a bucket of water over him.

Reg always said I could have been a decent fighter if I'd trained, but I think my performance against Adams that day surprised even him. The crowd was all over me offering congratulations as Ron walked over and handed us £500.

'Thanks, boys,' he said, 'you've just saved us a fortune.'

With the financial backing of the Krays, Adams had been slated to fight a very hard man called Hughie Burton from Doncaster. He was another contender for King of the Gypsies and, based on Donny's performance against me, would have murdered him. It would have cost the Krays a pile of cash. Instead, the fight was shelved, indefinitely.

When he came round, Adams was still trying to talk big. 'That was a lucky punch,' he said.

'It might have been,' I replied, 'but it floored you, you fucking bully. Who do you want to fight now, me, Paul or Danny?'

The 'Bull-shitter' didn't fancy a second round so we split the £500 three ways and got drunk.

Later, Roy Shaw beat Adams too. I wasn't surprised. Despite his huge reputation, he was all mouth and no trousers. Big men often are. They are so used to having it their way most of the time they start believing their own hype and think the world owes them a living.

I suppose I should have thanked the horse. It set me up on a nice earner. After beating Adams, every Tom, Dick and Harry wanted to take a piece of me home to their caravan and I was raking in the cash fighting gypsies. It wasn't always easy money. Some of those gypsy fighters were tough as nails, fought like cornered rats and made a right mess of my knuckles, but for a while I was the man to beat on the travellers' circuit.

Another time I was taking on a right head banger. We were somewhere in the Midlands, I forget where, and Danny Woollard was my number two again. I'd cut my right eye when an earlier opponent forgot he was wearing a ring and blood was streaming down my face, forcing me to keep wiping it away. It was slowing me down against this huge Jack the Lad who had started the bout dancing around and taunting me. I'd given him a good hiding and he was looking a bit green but still on his feet. We were fighting three-minute rounds and I knew the bell wasn't far off. Sod it, I could finish this easily in the second round after I'd sorted out my eye. With a clang on an upturned bucket, the referee signalled the end of the round. Turning away from laughing boy, I made for my corner to grab a mouthful of water and get Danny to wipe the blood away.

Suddenly, out of the corner of my good eye, I caught a shape behind me moving fast and a palpable gasp from the crowd. I jerked round and a ring post wielded by my opponent whistled millimetres past my nose. It was a hefty lump of wood and could have killed me if it had connected fully. What the fuck was he thinking? I dived away from his swing and grabbed the stave, pulling him off balance towards my feet. Fucking hell, that was a close-run thing. Every sinew was straining now, every second of every bar fight I'd ever been in came into play. Fighting like this was in my DNA.

Hurling the wood away, I pulled the c**t towards me and butted him under the chin with the top of my head. He stumbled backwards but managed to catch himself, his hands on the floor behind him. I kicked him in the face, knocking him on to his back. There was blood everywhere and he was spitting teeth as I crouched over him and started working his head and belly. I picked him up by his hair and carried on hitting him. I was fucking wild. It wasn't Queensberry Rules but he'd taken a massive liberty fighting dirty like that and now he was paying the price. It was over in a couple of minutes. I stalked back to my corner, leaving his pals to drag him from the ring.

CHAPTER SIX

'CAREER CRIMINALS OFTEN MAKE PRISON SOUND GLAMOROUS. IF YOU CAN'T DO THE TIME, DON'T DO THE CRIME AND ALL THAT RUBBISH. MAYBE WHEN YOU SPEND AS MUCH TIME BEHIND BARS AS SOME OF THEM, AND IT'S ALL YOU KNOW, PORRIDGE DOES SEEM EASY. THE TRUTH IS PRISON IS HELL, PURE AND SIMPLE, AS I WAS FAST LEARNING. BEATINGS WERE COMMON, BULLYING RIFE, AND THE GUARDS TURNED A BLIND EYE TO ALL BUT THE MOST BRUTAL ATTACKS WHILE TAKING BUNGS FOR SMUGGLING DRUGS, PORN AND LUXURIES...'

THE WRONG PLACE AT THE WRONG TIME

Soon after his release from borstal, my old adversary Johnny Seagers was hard at work – blagging security vans with his gang. Armed robbery was coming of age in the seventies. Access to serious shooters and the lure of easy money from security vans made blagging a number-one career move for a lot of wannabe hard men. Compared with nowadays, it was a piece of cake. No CCTV, explosive dye packages or tracking devices. The notes might be numbered sequentially if they were on their way to a bank, but they could be laundered easily enough over time.

Nothing was risk free but the rewards were high enough to convince more than a few villains, including Johnny and his mates, that blagging, the modern equivalent of 'stand and deliver', was the way forward.

Johnny's gang had a nice little number going. An insider was tipping them off about the movements of vans carrying used cash to post offices. They were well organised and planned their blags down to the last minute. Everyone had a job to do and they did it well. The money was split equally and the organisation was professional. No squealing to nearest and dearest either. Of course, it wasn't to last. Whether there was a tip-off, or someone said the wrong thing to the wrong person, the cops got wise. The straw that broke the camel's back as far as Seagers was concerned was a spectacular attack on a security van in Essex, where the truck was rammed off the road before its back doors were taken off with hooks chained to a tractor, and every last pound note stolen. The Flying Squad started kicking in doors all over the East End. They weren't messing around either. It was a case of knock, knock, smash, 'On your knees, sonny Jim, you're nicked'.

I was an ex-borstal boy with a growing reputation for the naughties and a known associate of Seagers. You didn't have to be the smartest plod to put two and two together and come up with five. Within days, I too had been arrested, charged with armed robbery, and remanded to Wormwood Scrubs, known simply as the Scrubs and one of Britain's most notorious prisons back then. In fact, I was innocent. It was another case of wrong place, wrong time for Micky G, and I was confident I wasn't going down despite what I knew would be superhuman efforts by the Old Bill to make the charges stick and stick good. As far as the cops were concerned, it was a case of 'co-operate or rot'. I didn't plan to do either.

Having said that, it was some of the toughest bird I ever did. I'd been held briefly in the Scrubs before being sent to borstal two years earlier, but it had got worse since then. For a while I thought I had hit rock bottom. The Scrubs was overcrowded and filthy, the guards were brutal and the regime as hard as nails. It stank, too. Three of us to a cell, packed in like sardines, and no toilet. On arrival, each prisoner was issued with a bucket with a screw top. We were locked up for 20 hours a day and the smell was unimaginable. When you undid your bucket, it literally made you vomit. It was so bad there were times when, even though I was in fact innocent, I honestly thought it must be time to go straight.

Career criminals often make prison sound glamorous. If you can't do the time, don't do the crime and all that rubbish.

Maybe when you spend as much time behind bars as some of them, and it's all you know, porridge does seem easy. The truth is prison is hell, pure and simple, as I was fast learning. Beatings were common, bullying rife, and the guards turned a blind eye to all but the most brutal attacks while taking bungs for smuggling drugs, porn and luxuries to those who could afford them, which didn't include me.

Each morning at 7am it was slopping-out time. We queued with our buckets to empty them into a big white sink on the prison landing. With the tap running, buckets would often splash an evil concoction of liquid shit and piss over other prisoners and fights were common. If anyone wanted a shit at night they would do it in a piece of newspaper and throw it out through the barred windows rather than go in their slop bucket. The next morning the so-called 'shit patrol' – a trusted inmate with a prison officer for protection – would walk round outside the walls collecting the parcels. They were always goody-goodies and most mornings they would get pelted with shit themselves if the screw looked the wrong way. That was one very good reason not to be a trustee if you ask me.

Inside, we were as good as anonymous. In our blue prison uniforms and prison shirts and with our hair cut short, we all looked the same. It was as regimented as the army. We ate the same terrible food, read the same dog-eared paperbacks and we almost certainly smelled the same. The Scrubs stank of sweat and stale bodies. Screws were referred to as Mister and prisoners by their surnames. There was none of the pampering that goes on inside jail these days. You were lucky to get a three-day-old paper to read let alone a TV or radio. Unsurprisingly, tensions ran high and there was always an atmosphere of barely suppressed violence. It didn't take long for it to spill over and involve me. I was ready and waiting.

An inmate known as a bit of a wannabe hard case tried to shove me aside when we were queuing up for slopping out on the prison landing in my block.

'Outta the way, Glückstad,' he snarled as he barrelled past me.

I'd barely slept. One of my cellmates had got his hands on a bottle of illicit booze the night before and kept me up with his snoring. So I was in no mood to let this wannabe show me up. Quick as a flash I stuck my leg out and pushed him hard from behind.

'Sorry, mate,' I called after him as he careered down the corridor, off balance and yelling like a stuck pig. 'Mind how you go.'

His bucket lid must've been unscrewed because it came flying. Unfortunately for him, he hadn't tossed his shit out of the window and the mixture, ripe by now after sitting all night in his cell, went everywhere. All over him, all over the enormous bloke in front of him and dripping through the steel mesh flooring on to the cons below. It was chaos and I was pissing myself laughing.

Before he could point a finger, the bloke he'd covered in shit booted him hard, grabbed his head and smashed it into the wall, leaving a trail of blood, snot and shit smeared down the gloss-white prison wall. He was out for the count as I stepped over him with my own bucket to empty it. Funnily enough, he never pushed past me again, or anyone else for that matter. And he wasn't quite so mouthy with a broken nose, 10 stitches in his top lip and his cheeks filled with cotton wool to soak up the blood where he'd bitten his cheek nearly through.

One bloke who never had any trouble was Graham Young, who'd been dubbed the 'Teacup Poisoner' by the papers after killing three people by lacing their food and drink with chemicals. Young, born in North London and just a year older than me, had been fascinated with poisons from a young age. He killed his stepmother in his teens and was sent to Broadmoor hospital. Now he was facing his second spell inside for murdering two workmates and putting 70 more in hospital.

He might have been infamous as Britain's worst poisoner but

I liked him. He was a quiet bloke who scared the other cons half to death. No one wanted Young near his cup of tea, that's for sure, and they were afraid to push him about in case he poisoned them.

However, we got on well and he used to joke about giving me something nice with my food to take my mind off prison.

'Not today, Graham, thanks,' I used to laugh at him, 'maybe tomorrow, mate, maybe tomorrow.'

After nine months on remand, I was acquitted at Knightsbridge Crown Court. Despite their best efforts, no doubt, the cops hadn't been able to provide a shred of evidence against me, and I was free again. Johnny's accomplices got sentences of up to 25 years for their part in the armed robberies. Johnny turned supergrass and got five years inside and a new identity and life somewhere up in the Northeast on his release.

Turning informer was the ultimate betrayal as a villain and guaranteed you a life of hell on the inside as a stinking grass – and violent retribution on the outside if your past ever caught up with you. That's why most lags avoided like the plague giving any information to the authorities.

Not Johnny Seagers. To this day, I have no idea what they had on him, or what pressure they used. But he cracked and grassed up all his gang. Prison was hard enough if you were an ordinary con, but being a grass meant you had to watch your back every second of the day or risk a knife in the ribs, glass in your food or an old-fashioned kicking. Only sex offenders had it worse.

People were shocked – 'Fuck me! Seagers has turned grass' – but, because he didn't set me up, I couldn't judge him. There would be enough people doing that without me steaming in, and I knew he hadn't fingered me.

'Yeah, I know Micky Glückstad. He's a nice bloke and we've had a few drinks together but he wasn't in our gang,' he told the police.

Johnny's failure to implicate me made no difference to the Old Bill. They'd taken me off the streets for nine months of my life I'd never get back and for them that was a success. They didn't care if I was found not guilty. In fact, they probably knew I wasn't guilty. That was how policing was then: hard and unforgiving. They would always object to bail and more often than not the magistrates would agree. Once you were inside they had time to turn the screws and get you for something – anything. You couldn't complain and you didn't. You knew that was the path you walked as a hard man. It was the law of the jungle, if you like. Sometimes you won, often you lost. This time I'd lost nine months but, ultimately, had come up smelling of roses.

As far as I know, Johnny is still alive. But he isn't Johnny Seagers any more. Once he turned grass, he gave up his whole previous life. They give you a new name, fresh National Insurance number, and a new home in a different part of the country with friends and neighbours who know nothing of your past. To all intents and purposes, you disappear. Johnny's family moved away from the East End too. Life would have been intolerable for them. It's very hard to find someone when they change their name and their life. The biggest problem for an old con is staying straight. But as far as I know Seagers managed it. If he had been tracked down, it would have been all over. There were a lot of very heavy people in the East End and a grass wouldn't last long. Johnny's gang received very heavy sentences and there were a lot of very unhappy people picking up the pieces.

While Johnny and his gang were sent down, I was delighted to be out. No more slopping out. No more grief from the screws and no more Graham Young and his killer tea. My idle daydreams about going straight went right out the window. I'd served my time and watched my mum weep as I was carted away in handcuffs. This time, I vowed to myself as the court doors banged shut behind me and I avoided the evil glares of the coppers outside, it would be different.

As usual, it was straight back into trouble.

I went straight out drinking with my old pal Danny Woollard – who later got eight years for handling £7 million worth of stolen bearer bonds from the notorious Snowhill robbery – to celebrate my freedom. We were in a club called the Hathaway that Danny owned at the time when a nutter we all knew called Martin Dunn started kicking off with the old bloke taking the money at the door. Now Dunn was one hard c**t. He had a terrible scar down his face from where he'd been slashed in prison. He'd recently bested three men in a fight at the Star pub in Manor Park, but here he was beating the crap out of an old bloke whose only offence had been to ask for the entrance fee.

It was bang out of order, and I started to take my jacket off to intervene before things got too nasty for the old boy as he desperately looked around for help.

'Not so fast, Micky,' piped up Danny. 'You've only been out a few hours. You leave this to me.'

Well, you don't want to get in the way of a man and his mission so I took a swig of my pint and sat back down to enjoy the show. Danny was very tasty back then, built like the proverbial brick shithouse. But Dunn was no slouch either and the pair of them had a tremendous battle on the floor of the club, sending chairs, tables and the odd punter flying.

It was a proper dust-up but Dunn ended up slumped over an upturned chair with a broken nose, broken ribs and blood pouring from his head. Dunn's mates couldn't believe Danny had beaten him and started moving in menacingly.

I jumped up, threw down my jacket and asked them straight up: 'Right, lads, who's next?' Gesturing to their comatose mate, I continued: 'If you want some of that, you're in the right place. OK, what will it be?'

I had no takers. Bricking themselves, they grabbed Dunn under the armpits and dragged him groaning out of the club. We sat back down to finish our drinks as the sound of sirens drew near. Yes, I thought, taking a deep swig of my lager and pulling my jacket back on, it was good to be free again. But I didn't know how long it would last with the way my luck was going. Funnily enough, when the police turned up, Dunn was lying unconscious by the roadside. He woke up long enough to start fighting them, and promptly got nicked.

A week or so later, I was drinking with a friend when he introduced me to his pal, Jimmy Boyle, who was on the run from a murder charge in Scotland. I met Jimmy at the British Lion pub in Stratford during the lunchtime rush. The pub was filling with workers from nearby factories and doing a roaring trade.

Jimmy, who always denied killing anyone, told me London was a good place to lose yourself, and said the Krays had set him up in a nice flat.

'If you're not known, London's a safe place,' he laughed.

I wasn't so sure.

As I was waiting to buy a round, I saw one of the barmen discreetly unbolting the side door. My sixth sense was screaming. As the door opened, I saw a police van backing up. Suddenly, a dozen or so armed cops stormed the pub. They had come for Jimmy, and there were too many to fight. He knew the game was up but struggled bravely, before being dragged in handcuffs out of the pub.

After a couple of minutes, the cops left – a mixture of the Met and their Scottish cousins – the pub returned to normal and drinking resumed. It wasn't so unusual in the East End to see the police banging someone into a van, sadly.

Jimmy was found guilty of the murder of William 'Babs' Rooney and sentenced to life imprisonment at the toughest Scottish jail, Barlinnie prison, where he reinvented himself as an artist. Today he's married and happy. Good luck to him.

I didn't know it then, but later on the British Lion would again feature dramatically in my life.

Not a month had passed before I was back in front of the

Old Bill facing a proper fit-up. A 40-foot articulated lorry full of whisky had been stolen from a distribution warehouse in Purfleet, Essex. Two blokes had walked in with the paperwork, signed for it, taken the keys and literally driven it away right under the noses of the owners. The cops fancied Danny and yours truly as the guilty parties. No doubt by the time I got hauled in, the booze had been split into cases and sold under the counter to pubs and off-licences across London.

It sounded like such a nice little earner I half wished I had been in on it as I sat in Basildon police station loudly proclaiming my innocence to my solicitor. By now I was a pro when facing the cops. Say nothing, admit to nothing, and deny everything. It was simple as long as you didn't let them rile you. And they tried. This time round I actually forgot I was innocent. That wouldn't have stopped them giving me three years. A collar was a collar as far as the police were concerned. So I was saying nothing. As long as you were polite, you could usually avoid having your head smashed into the interview-room table – especially with the country cops, as we liked to think of the Essex Constabulary. The Met, they weren't.

'Your name is Michael Glückstad?'

'No comment, sir.'

'Solicitor, please tell your client we know who he is and he's wasting everyone's time refusing to speak.'

Me: 'No comment.'

In the end, they had to let Danny and me loose. The fellow who accepted the load sheets couldn't identify us as the pair of thieves. The cops were obviously bitterly disappointed but I was free again and, given we hadn't boosted the booze lorry, in dire need of cash.

CHAPTER SEVEN

'ROY WAS HUGE. HE LOOMED OVER ME, STARING ME OUT. I LOOKED DEEP INTO THE DEVIL'S EYES AND SAW ONLY DARKNESS. HE WAS TRULY ALARMING IN THE FLESH. HE HAD WEIGHED IN AT ABOUT THREE STONE HEAVIER THAN ME AND WAS PUMPED UP FROM HIS TIME SPENT LIFTING WEIGHTS IN PRISON. EVERY SINEW WAS STRAINING AND HIS VEINS STOOD OUT LIKE KNOTTED ROPE OVER BULGING MUSCLES...'

GETTING UGLY WITH THE PRETTY BOY

With his massive forearms and fists pumping like pistons and his face contorted into a terrible snarl of rage, Roy Shaw was a truly terrifying prospect. His nickname might have been 'Pretty Boy' but, from where I was standing, back to the ropes and fending off a flurry of blows as I struggled to breathe, he looked like a grumpy bulldog licking piss off a nettle. His small, pig-like eyes sunk into his face and his brow furrowed as he concentrated hard on trying to batter me senseless in front of a hyped-up and baying capacity crowd at Dagenham Working Men's Club.

Shaw was famous for the strength of his body blows – proper rib-breakers – and I was hunched up tight, trying to protect my chest with my arms and elbows. Bigger men than me had felt their bones snap under the onslaught of Shaw's fists. So, when he dropped his guard for a split second, I saw my opportunity and sprang forward. Moving like a greased whippet, I pulled my right fist back and launched a sweeping roundhouse blow to his head, catching him above his left eye and drawing a huge roar of approval from the crowd. Roy reeled back, a surprised look in his eyes, and I followed with a hard left jab to the chin, just catching his square jaw. Now I was pressing forward, forcing him back towards his corner, darting and jabbing, testing his defences. Roy had come at me on the first bell like a freight train, looking for the quick knockout. Now I could see him reappraising me.

I was back in a proper boxing ring for the first time since I had trained with Reg Kray at the Double R club as a teenager and I had been forced to fight Roy in gloves to satisfy the management. For a prizefighter like me, it was like swimming in a three-piece suit. Nonetheless, we were toe to toe and trading blows like two men possessed, neither giving an inch. In his bestselling autobiography, *Pretty Boy*, Roy described me as a mongrel from the East End. 'I beat him in three rounds,' he wrote. 'It was stopped because he was taking too much punishment.'

The way I saw it could not be more different. I believe to this day that I bested Shaw and people who were ringside that night still describe it as one of the greatest amateur bouts they ever saw. Quite simply, we fought each other to a standstill and then some. If I was a mongrel, then Roy got bit, bad. For Shaw, it was once bitten, twice shy. We never fought again after our epic match, although I followed his career and would have taken him any time if the price was right.

Growing up in Stepney, 12 years older than me, Shaw was hard as the cobbles beneath his feet and enjoyed an unrivalled reputation as a ruthless bastard. He lost his dad young and was always fighting, mainly when he was drunk. Roy was reckoned in the East End as a man not to be crossed. It was only when he finished a 12-year stretch for armed robbery that he took up prizefighting. He'd been a talented schoolboy boxer, but a criminal record is fatal to a licence and when the law caught up with him it ruined his career in the licensed ring. Now he was nearly 40 and it took guts to put on the gloves against men 20 years younger. But he was in good condition, having used his time behind bars and in Broadmoor high-security hospital to train hard. Over the years I met many men who would describe themselves as merciless, but Roy was a different category of psychopath. He was utterly without a moral compass. Only one thing truly mattered in life to Roy Shaw and that was Roy.

In his own words, written in the comfortable retirement he'd looked unlikely ever to live to enjoy, he admitted: 'Doctors said I was unpredictable, uncontrollable and, worse still, unjustifiably violent. I admit I have no conscience, nor pity. If that makes me mad then I'm barking.'

Despite this, or maybe because of it, he was a breathtaking fighter and, with the help of promoter Joey Pyle, a close friend of the Krays, his unlicensed boxing career began to take off. Joey selected Roy's opponents and sorted the money and publicity. Roy turned up like a shift worker and did the business in the ring. He had two great assets as a fighter. He could take enormous punishment without flinching and he was a ferocious body puncher, splintering ribs and hammering his opponents. These included Lew 'Wild Thing' Yates, Lenny McLean and American Ron Stander, a serious fighter who'd challenged Joe Frazier for the heavyweight championship of the world.

I first came across Roy in the social club of the Plessey engineering firm in Ilford, East London, when he was working the door. I'd heard a bit about him on the grapevine. In the local vernacular, he was supposed to be able to have a bit of a fight. He was staggeringly drunk and his squinty little eyes were having trouble focusing. The thing about Roy was that he was a fine fighter and a quiet, sociable bloke when sober but a paralytic and dangerous boozer. When he was hammered, he was a pile of trouble but a child could probably have put him down. Not that I'd have recommended trying even at the best of times.

Another time, my pal Danny Woollard faced him down in the Greyhound pub in Chadwell Heath. Danny and a pal had been trying to pull a couple of girls when Roy, legless and staggering, started making snide comments. When the girls went to freshen up, Roy told Danny and his mate: 'Right, lads, time for you to go home as me and my pal are going to keep your girlfriends company.'

Danny was not a shrinking violet and looked at Shaw in astonishment. He recalled: 'I started to laugh. I really thought he was joking. But one look at his stern face and I knew he meant it. I said, "Roy – that's your name, isn't it? You ought to be on the stage, telling fucking jokes like that." He started hollering and hooting. Then he just sauntered away, mumbling. But he had ruined our night. When I turned round the girls had left.'

Danny had told me this story so there was no love lost between us when we finally met in the ring. My reputation as a tidy fighter was growing and Joey was looking for challengers to build Shaw's name and the size of the purse he could command. He had a clever strategy. Roy's opponents were all muscular brawlers but never too young or too talented. Roy was strong, but against a really fast and skilful youngster he might have struggled. Instead, he was earning a fortune having proper tear-ups with blokes who had seen better days themselves. Don't get me wrong, Roy himself would have fought anyone, but he liked the money he was earning and trusted his advisers. Whatever his faults, he was a great showman who never let the crowd down. He would boogie into the ring to blaring music and dance around, whipping the fans into a frenzy long before such routines became popular at mainstream bouts.

Joey Pyle had failed to secure Davy Elmore, a nasty piece of work, for Roy. Davy had told them: 'I will fight you right now in the car park but I have never been in a boxing ring or worn a pair of boxing gloves.'

Next they tried me. I'd just come out of custody and was celebrating my freedom with a good drink in Twilights on Stratford Broadway when Roy walked in to challenge me midway through the evening.

For once the big man kept quiet and let the brains do the talking. Joey offered a purse of £2,000, a very decent sum of money for an evening's work and a tempting offer, as I was skint. But fighting was the last thing on my mind, way behind getting drunk and, if I could get lucky, getting laid. After a recent run of bad luck, I didn't have two coins to rub together for my stake.

'I haven't got two bob to my name,' I told them.

Then an old friend, Alan Sewell, stepped in. 'I'll back you, Mick,' he said.

'OK, let's step outside, gents,' I said.

But Joey wasn't grooming his boy to take part in car-park dust-ups. Where was the sense in that? He suggested we meet at the Seven Kings Hotel in Ilford in three weeks' time so they could whip up interest and sell some tickets. I agreed. Fuck it. He looked the business in his double-breasted suit, but I was pretty certain I could do Roy Shaw if anyone could. I knew his reputation – everyone did – but I'd won a fair few fights and didn't fear anyone.

As it was, half of the East End turned up on the night. Word had got round that I was going to fight the Pretty Boy and it had drawn a big crowd. It had also drawn the police, who'd heard there was a big bare-knuckle brawl going down and came out mob-handed to nick everyone. So we had to cancel. There were a lot of angry punters, but it built up even more hype. The Old Bill sniffed around me a bit too, but it didn't bother me. I think they were as keen to see the fight as everyone else, as long as it was above board and refereed.

I'd like to say I spent the extra week training, but in all probability I was out on the lash as usual. I hadn't trained seriously since I was 16, and even then I'd just been messing. I never fancied the endurance training or pad work that is the bread and butter of a career fighter. The only time I really exercised was when I was behind bars to stop me going barking mad. It didn't suit my style. A lot of people told me later I could have made a proper living out of boxing if I'd taken it seriously and trained. That wasn't my game at all. I enjoyed a tear-up but practising would've been too much like hard work, even with two grand on the table against Roy Shaw. I laid off the booze the night before to keep my head clear. In my book, that was as much preparation as I'd need ahead of fighting Shaw.

A week later, having sold at least 500 tickets, we reconvened in the main function room at Dagenham Working Men's Club. It was packed with punters, jammed round the boxing ring, and the bar was doing a roaring trade. Both Roy and myself had dozens of friends and supporters along to cheer us on. The plan was that it should be a bare-knuckle fight but on the night Roy's side claimed we'd all get nicked if we went at it without the gloves.

Roy's man Joey came into the dressing room to tell me: 'Micky, there are a few police in the audience who will close us down unless you wear these gloves.'

'What fucking gloves?' I asked.

I'd never worn gloves since I was a teenager but I agreed reluctantly. I was so eager to put Shaw on his back and collect my two grand. I was worried a bit about losing my punching power but, fuck it, I was ready for the battle.

Then, another of Shaw's advisers came to see me. He said: 'We've heard you fight dirty. If you start any of that, Roy will tear your head off.'

It couldn't have psyched me up better if I'd been paying them to get me in the right frame of mind. I quickly replied: 'Tell Roy that if he wants it that way I'll get in the ring and take my fucking gloves off and – see this finger?' I held my right index finger to the bloke. 'I will stick it in his eye and pull his eyeball out of his fucking head. Otherwise, we'll fight like men.'

There was a stony silence as Roy's man went back to his boss. As the door closed I pissed myself laughing. Maybe there was a splash of nerves there too. I'd never fought before such a crowd and I didn't want to let myself down.

A couple of minutes later he was back. 'Look, Mick, the place is crawling with Old Bill so keep it cool,' he said. 'They'd love to shut us down and there'll be a riot if this fight doesn't take place tonight.'

'All right, as long as Roy does,' I replied. 'He's got the reputation for going nuts, not me. I just want my cash.'

The legendary Nosher Powell was warming up the crowd. He shouted his customary 'Bring on the lions' as I made my way into the ring. Ever the showman, Roy waited until I was in my corner before shadow-boxing into the room to a full-volume recording of Gary Glitter singing 'C'mon C'mon'. The atmosphere was electric and the place exploded. I could feel the hairs on the back of my neck standing up as Roy clambered into the ring, staring me out with his demonic eyes. Then he was jumping about, stirring up the crowd and waving to his supporters. He looked the biz. By contrast, I wasn't well kitted out. My gloves had been lent to me by Joey Pyle and didn't fit very well and I'd not bandaged my hands. I had no gum shield and was in borrowed trainers, shorts and a singlet, swigging from a bottle of lemonade to keep myself hydrated. I looked a muppet, but that could be an advantage. Roy wouldn't expect to meet a fighter when the bell rang.

Billy Gibney was my corner man for the night. For once, he was bricking himself. As Roy arrived, he looked over at me and said: 'Mick, I'm glad you're fighting him and not me.' Then he jumped out of the ring and disappeared.

The crowd was baying for blood so Nosher called us to the centre of the ring and warned us to fight fair. As we touched gloves, I don't think anyone in the place would've given me much of a chance. Roy was huge. He loomed over me, staring me out. I looked deep into the devil's eyes and saw only darkness. He was truly alarming in the flesh. He had weighed in at about three stone heavier than me and was pumped up from his time spent lifting weights in prison. Every sinew was straining and his veins stood out like knotted rope over bulging muscles. Knowing his reputation for dishing out monster body blows, my granddad's advice from my days shadow-boxing in his front room came to me.

'You've got to take the punishment as well as dishing it out, son,' he'd told me all those years ago. 'You'll never win if you can't soak it up just as well as you can dish it out.' Good old Granddad, his advice never went out of date.

I glanced around the crowd. All around were screaming faces. They couldn't wait to see the Pretty Boy give me a hiding. I turned back to Roy and laughed in his face. The bell rang for round one and Roy came at me hard and fast. We were toe to toe, trading good, strong blows to the body and head, testing each other.

For all Roy's showmanship and vanity, he wasn't a stupid fighter. He was probing hard, landing a flurry of blows then pulling back to keep something in reserve. For my part, I didn't know about pacing myself and was giving it all I had, dodging and weaving and going for Roy's face and head when I saw a chance. It was tiring me out quickly. But I could see Roy puffing away too and I was doing my best to avoid his body blows. A couple caught me hard in the stomach. It wasn't a myth: the bloke could punch like a freight train and I knew I'd have to watch it or I'd be on my back with cracked ribs or a collapsed lung.

Suddenly, I saw an opening, and socked Roy with a roundhouse to the head followed by a couple of sharp jabs to the chin. Bang. Bang. Bang. I could see the shock in his little piggy eyes.

'How dare this little c**t come into my ring and hit me?' he seemed to be saying. Then, a shadow of doubt clouded them: 'What if he hits me like that again?'

I gave him a big grin and danced away. The crowd was going bananas. Roy made a last lunge at me and we batted at each other, waiting for the bell to ring. Dong. Three minutes gone, and one round down. We returned to our corners to a huge roar of approval. The crowd knew they were watching something special. I was soaked in sweat as I took a pull from my bottle of lemonade. I couldn't sit down, so I danced about a bit to stop myself seizing up, waving to mates in the crowd. Out of the corner of my eye, I could see Roy's mates looking a bit worried. They'd expected him to come straight out and give me a proper lamping and I'd soaked up everything he threw at me. Easy meat I was not.

To my knowledge there's only one photograph in existence of the fight. I'm bending down protecting my body to the left of the picture as Roy hammers my ribs with his right fist, face curled from the effort. The snap is grainy and out of focus but it catches the essence of the fight perfectly. You can see how powerfully physical a fighter Roy was compared to me. He wasn't used to anyone surviving his onslaught – bigger men had been bested in seconds – and it undermined his otherwise supreme confidence when I refused to bend to his will.

The second and third rounds followed the same pattern. Roy came out swinging and I soaked up the blows I couldn't avoid while giving a decent account of myself in return. Each of us was trying to dominate the ring, neither giving a lesson in technique. It was fast becoming survival of the fittest. Who could stay upright longest? Who could soak up the most grief? With all the odds in his favour – size, weight and power – Roy still couldn't floor me and we were both tiring fast. I could see a vein throbbing in his temple like a beacon. It gave me something to aim for under the lashing of sweat rolling down his face and chest as we slugged backwards and forwards.

By round four, I had my back to the ropes and was taking a beating but still refusing to go down. Now I could see real uncertainty in Roy's eyes. Despite his best efforts, he hadn't been able to hurt me and he didn't know why. Many times Shaw had sent professional fighters crashing to the canvas crying under this sort of punishment yet this East End toerag,

Micky Glückstad, was still on his feet and hitting back. He couldn't make sense of it. Dong. Another round down.

By the time we were five rounds in, Roy could barely stand but was still punching hard. I was exhausted too, laughing at Roy's efforts and enraging him further. The bell rang again and it was back to our corners, fighting for breath.

The atmosphere inside the club was fetid. The place was awash with booze, and condensation and sweat were dripping from the windows and ceiling like a spring shower. Smoke from a thousand fags lingered round the ring like smog, stinging our eyes and catching in our throats.

For some reason the timekeeper dallied between rounds five and six. There was a longer break and the crowd was urging him to ring the bell and set us at each other's throat again like the wild dogs we were. I was slumped back against the ropes trying to catch my breath. I could barely move. But, when it did go, I pulled myself back to my feet and lurched forward. Roy looked like a zombie. His eyes were dull. He was punched out.

In fairness, I'd not hurt him badly, though I had scored some good hits. He had worn himself down trying to destroy me and his phenomenal strength was running out. If I could keep on my feet for a few more minutes, I reckoned he might collapse. Now I wasn't even fighting back, just soaking up the blows, which by now didn't have much power, and trying to catch my breath. Danny Woollard and another dozen or so of my mates had jumped on to the ring apron and were screaming at me to keep going. If I could keep standing I'd win. I was certain. As round six was ending, Roy and I were gripping each other in a boxer's clasp.

Suddenly, the ref stopped the fight. I thought I'd won. So did the crowd. Roy slumped forward and grunted at me, 'I don't want a rematch.'

It was complete chaos but other people heard him say that, including Danny Woollard, who had jumped into the ring as the bell went. The crowd was boozed up and going wild, but no verdict had been announced. Everyone assumed I had beaten Roy Shaw – his first defeat. He was practically carried out of the ring and limped back to his dressing room.

Before I could celebrate, I went to see the promoter to get my winnings. He laughed at me: 'What money? You lost.'

I couldn't believe it. 'How did I lose when I never went down?' I asked. 'A prizefight is last man standing and Roy had to be helped out of the ring. I was still there and still standing. I won.'

The promoter told me: 'This was a boxing match and your corner threw in the towel.'

'What fucking corner? I never had a corner so how could they have thrown it in?' I was livid now. My blood was running cold in my veins with anger and I told him in no uncertain terms: 'I want my fucking money now.'

'There's no money,' he replied, backing away. 'Roy's side have taken it.'

I nearly chinned the bloke there and then. Instead, I asked where I could find Roy. The promoter told me Shaw had gone straight down to the Epping Forest Country Club, a converted former stately home at Woolston Manor, in Chigwell, to celebrate his victory. What a fucking liberty taker. With Danny, Billy and some other mates in tow for muscle, I jumped in a cab and headed down to the club to confront Roy.

Outside the club, I asked the bouncers: 'Is Roy Shaw in tonight?'

'Yes, mate. He's inside celebrating winning a prizefight.'

'Get the fucker out here now,' I demanded.

I wouldn't go in. This was for the cobbles. Finally, after some fannying about, Roy came out. He was at least 10-handed and wearing a dark-brown suit but his face looked bruised and puffy. He was still knackered but had a beer in his hand.

I told him: 'You haven't beaten me yet, Roy. Let's finish it here and now. Just you and me.'

I could see him thinking hard. Even though he had 10 blokes with him, I don't think he fancied his chances. I was raging and my mates were a boozed-up mob spoiling for trouble. Finally, he laughed and said: 'Do me a favour, Mick. I don't think either of us won, to be honest.'

Then, to be fair to him, he shoved a bundle of notes at me and went back inside. Taking his lead, some of Roy's pals had a whip-round and handed me another bundle of money. By the end I had £3,000 so I was well pleased. We would never be friends but respect had been maintained on both sides. I relaxed my battered body and went inside for a drink.

To this day, people still talk about those first two or three rounds of pure adrenalin as one of the greatest battles ever. It was certainly my ultimate fight, in or out of the ring, and one of the hardest ever.

Later, Roy fought Lenny 'The Guv'nor' McLean for a £20,000 purse in a Croydon nightclub called Cinatra's, where I'd once taken on a heavyweight called Terry Sharp who both Shawy and McLean had sidestepped. Terry was a real pro and a very hard bloke. I managed to take him to six rounds before the referee, Nosher Powell again, called it a draw. We were both satisfied with that, I think.

I'd beaten Lenny in a bare-knuckle brawl when he was a lunatic who'd have a go at anyone. Like me, he'd never trained seriously, and relied on his sheer size to overwhelm his rivals. Now he stood in the ring goading his opponent, shouting, 'Come on, Roy, try and put me down.'

After one round he was knackered and stopped defending himself. After three rounds, the fight was stopped and Shaw pronounced the winner by the referee even though he hadn't floored McLean.

When they met again, McLean was a different man. He'd been training hard and was toned and fit. This time it was a properly matched contest, and the 13 or so years he had on Roy made a big difference. The venue was Cinatra's again and it was packed. In round one McLean sent Roy practically flying through the ropes and out of the ring. It was the hardest punch I've ever seen.

Roy looked like he'd been hit with a sledgehammer. As Roy's seconds carried him all but sparko back into the ring, McLean started jumping around, trying to kick him. It was really dangerous now. One of Roy's mates, Joe Carrington, who must've had nerves of steel, jumped into the ring and pushed McLean away, squaring up to him. The crowd were going crazy but before anything nastier could happen the bell rang. Roy was finished.

His corner tried to get him back into the fight but that was it. It was game over for Roy and a devastating defeat. McLean stood at the side of the ring, screaming into the crowd: 'I'm the guv'nor now. I'm the guv'nor now. Who's the guv'nor? I'm the guv'nor.' Roy had been a favourite but the crowd lapped it up. That was how the McLean legend was born. Even after his defeat, Roy carried on fighting and making money. Good luck to him, though. He was a fearsome opponent and deserved a happy retirement, even though he was a hard man to like and sometimes a bully.

Joey Pyle, who remained a close associate of the Krays until their deaths, even acting as Ronnie's best man when he married in Broadmoor in 1985, was jailed for 14 years in 1992 for running a multimillion-pound drug racket.

An Old Bailey jury, who had to be given 24-hour protection to stop them being nobbled, heard he had been at the top of Scotland Yard's wanted list for years, cheating justice for three decades before the law finally caught up with him.

it was picked. In round one McCann sent Roy practically flying through the ropes and out of the ring. It was [illegible] much [illegible]

Roy hooked McCann [illegible] with a sledgehammer. As soon as [illegible] turned him all [illegible] back into the ring, McCann started jumping around [illegible]. It was really dangerous now. One of Roy's [illegible] Joe Carrington, who [illegible] and pushed McCann away [illegible] [illegible] Roy was banned.

[illegible] back [illegible] right [illegible] [illegible] McCann [illegible] [illegible] [illegible] [illegible] [illegible] [illegible] [illegible] [illegible] [illegible] [illegible] wasn't a [illegible] [illegible] a hard [illegible] sometimes a bully.

[illegible] a [illegible] of the [illegible] [illegible] [illegible] [illegible] [illegible] [illegible] [illegible]

[illegible] [illegible] [illegible] caught up with him.

CHAPTER EIGHT

'I REALISED I'D BEEN STABBED IN THE ARM BY ANOTHER OF THE BOUNCERS AND WAS LOSING BLOOD OVER MY NEW WHITE SHIRT. FIVE AGAINST ONE AND THEY STILL NEEDED A KNIFE IN A PUNCH-UP. FUCKING PUSSIES. I WAS FADING FAST AND TOOK A KICKING BEFORE I MANAGED TO DRAG MYSELF AWAY AND PERSUADE A PARKED-UP BLACK-CAB DRIVER TO TAKE ME TO HOSPITAL...'

SHOOT-OUT AT THE TWO PUDDINGS

The pump-action shotgun was cold and menacing. The dark metal of the barrel gleamed in the passing streetlights and it looked bloody terrifying. I'd oiled the action and tried it half a dozen times to make sure it was smooth and reliable, slipping off to Epping Forest to test-fire the gun. Now it was loaded and sitting heavy in my lap alongside a balaclava in the passenger seat of a stolen Mercedes taking the backstreets to avoid unnecessary attention from the Old Bill. My pockets were loaded with spare shells; this time I was going to war.

Guns had always been easy to come by if you knew the right man. Lugers, Colts and Smith and Wesson revolvers had arrived back with demobbed servicemen in their tens of thousands after the war and could be picked up, no questions asked, for as little as a fiver. If you needed a bit more bang for your buck there was always someone who could get his hands on an army surplus Sten machine gun and even grenades.

I never held much truck with weapons. I'd always avoided going tooled up, preferring to use my fists to settle scores like a man, or sometimes carrying a small cosh or a bottle of squirt up my sleeve if I needed a bit more protection. Some villains saw guns like a brickie might his trowel or hod, as a piece of professional equipment to be used carefully and professionally to scare the living daylights out of whoever they were pointed at.

Others were simply nutters who didn't care who they shot. If you got in their sights, so be it. It's called collateral damage nowadays; back then, an innocent being caught in the crossfire caused moral outrage on both sides of the law. But shootings were still fairly rare.

The Shepherd's Bush killings of three policemen by Harry Roberts and two accomplices in 1966 sparked a national manhunt and became infamous because they were so unusual. Talking about the killings, Roberts, whose policy was to leave no witnesses, admitted: 'We shot them because they were going to nick us and we didn't want to go to jail for 15 years. We were professional criminals. We don't react the same way as ordinary people. The police aren't like real people to us. They're strangers; they're the enemy.'

Hearing that, it's no surprise to me that Roberts is still inside and one of Britain's longest-serving prisoners. And I don't agree. To me, that spells psycho and, whatever else I may have been, I wasn't a nutter. I didn't like the police, sure, but, until they started shooting at me, I wasn't going to start firing back. Today's kids will kill someone for treading on their toe in a busy bar or to steal a pair of trainers. It's a tragedy. Back in my day that sort of thing would be settled with fists and a handshake afterwards. No one wanted a murder charge on his head either. The ultimate sanction for taking a life – the death penalty – wasn't even abolished until 1969, when I was 21.

So I had to shake my head and wonder if this time I'd really lost the plot when I found myself barrelling through East London in the passenger seat of a black Mercedes clutching a fully loaded pump-action shotgun like my life depended on it. Billy Gibney was driving and three mates who had come along for the ride – one of the East End's first drive-by shootings – were sitting in the back as Bill threw the sporty motor around like Stirling Moss.

'Take it easy, Billy,' I muttered. 'Let's not get nicked before we do anything.'

'Sorry, Mick,' he replied, easing the speed slightly, but still gripping the steering wheel white-knuckled and looking shit-scared.

I knew how he felt this time, I really did. What the fuck were we up to? I hated shooters. I hated them. The madness had begun 24 hours earlier in the Two Puddings pub in Stratford, East London. It was a traditional spit-and-sawdust establishment, known by some as the Butcher's Shop because of the blood that was always being spilled there, but I liked it. There was a bar out front and a club upstairs – the Devil's Kitchen – and it was popular with the stars. The Krays, the Small Faces and the footballer Bobby Moore, whose own pub was nearby, were all regulars at one time or another. At that time, the Puddings was owned by Big Kenny Johnson – a huge man with a hard reputation who wouldn't stand for any trouble. His son Matt was a talented young musician who later found fame in the band The The. The only time Kenny's doormen got musical was when they were pounding out beats on the skulls of troublemakers. They were rock hard and always up for a tumble.

As has often been the case, it was the demon drink that did for me that night. I'd obviously had one too many sherbets and for some reason was spoiling for a fight after going on a solitary pub crawl out of boredom. As anyone will testify, I've never looked for trouble. But when it comes I have never shied away. I'd started the night at the Swan in Stratford, another traditional boozer favoured by villains, then headed to the Puddings after sinking half a dozen pints.

Big Kenny was standing inside the door with four or five minders hanging about like sharply suited Neanderthals. Kenny was a real flash Harry with a mouth in proportion to his size.

'Piss off, Glückstad, you're not welcome here,' he snarled.

'Charmed, I'm sure,' I laughed at him. 'You're a very big man with five minders. How about just you and me try it on?'

Before I could make a move, I was surrounded by all five of the fuckers. Built like gorillas and with matching personal hygiene, they weren't taking any chances.

My heart told me I needed to beat the crap out of my man, and then take on his mates too, but my head, still functioning despite the booze I'd sunk, told me I'd get slaughtered if I tried to take them all on at once. Even with steam blowing out of my nostrils I knew I could be in a right old pickle.

But I wasn't walking away. The red mist had descended and I was eyeing a nearby table for an empty glass I could grab if things got nasty. Pulling myself up to my full height of five foot ten and trying to make myself look as imposing as possible, I told them: 'I can't fight you together but I'll take you one at a time. If you want to take me down, do it like men. Not a bunch of pansies.'

Big Kenny laughed in my face: 'I've never been beat, little man.'

To be fair to Kenny, he must've been 10 years older than me but no one had ever beaten him in a fight and he was fit and strong. Fast too. Before I had time to take my jacket off, his fist crashed into my jaw like a hammer. He followed with a left to my head and a right hook to my ribcage. I was reeling. The left hit me pretty high on the cheekbone, a ring on his finger drawing blood. Seeing the hook to my ribs coming, I deflected it with my elbow.

Now he was overconfident and wide open and I was gaining momentum. I feinted with my left shoulder and, as he drew away, I slammed my right fist into his nose, feeling it crunch beneath my knuckles as he went down gasping like a suffocating man. He came up on to his knees but he was wobbly and struggled to get up. Before he could pull himself upright, I kneed him in the face. He went down again and this time stayed down.

Two of the minders came at me fast but I was properly angry now. I lashed out left and right at one, knocking the first out sparko before being beaten from all sides by the bunch of cowards. I was trying to clear some space when something hard caught my upper right arm. Suddenly, it wasn't functioning like it was supposed to – dishing out pain and retribution. I realised I'd been stabbed in the arm by another of the bouncers and was losing blood over my new white shirt.

Five against one and they still needed a knife in a punch-up. Fucking pussies. I was fading fast and took a kicking before I managed to drag myself away and persuade a parked-up black-cab driver to take me to hospital. A doctor at Queen Mary's took one look at my bruised and battered face and said nothing but raised his eyebrows. I didn't want the police involved; I'd be sorting this out myself. 'I got jumped in the street by muggers. I didn't see their faces,' I told him. 'They got me from behind.'

I gave a false name and address so it didn't matter if he believed me or not. More often than not, the hospitals would grass you to the Old Bill if they could get away with it. But in the middle of the graveyard shift at a busy A&E, the last thing he needed was trouble.

Joking, I told him: 'As far as you're concerned, mate, I leaned on a knife that happened to be passing.'

He stitched me up, gave me some painkillers and I was out. No questions asked, thank you very much.

I was still young and a quick healer. My wound stitched together nicely and before the month was out I was doing push-ups and dumb-bell curls to strengthen my arm. To this day it hurts when the weather gets cold, but that's life. Once I was back on my feet I wanted to get even with the leery gits who'd knifed me.

I couldn't risk getting lifted by going in mob-handed. That was how I came to be barrelling through the East End like Al Capone in a fast car with a balaclava over my face and two ponies' (£50) worth of shooter cradled in my lap. I was lucky. The Johnson brothers, including my pal Kenny, were hanging around outside the door of the pub as usual as we roared up.

Aiming high, I pumped shells into the windows, showering the c**ts with glass and sending them diving on to the pavement, before we screeched off around the block. But I wasn't satisfied. I was fired up and wanted to cause them more trouble. I still had tons of shells in my pockets, too.

'Go round again, Billy,' I ordered.

'Are you mad, Mick?' he asked.

'Just do it, mate.'

The police were already outside when we steamed up again and pumped more shells into the Puddings, blowing out the few remaining windows.

I was laughing like a maniac but I never aimed to hit anyone. Then we were off again like a bat out of hell, tyres burning. The car went up in flames in a derelict warehouse on the Isle of Dogs and the gun went into the river. It had been a good night's work. No one was hurt – though I think a copper might have got a cut ear from flying glass – and a message had been delivered: don't fuck with Micky Glückstad. Although the Johnsons had plenty of enemies, they would suspect me but they would never go to the authorities with their information.

The next day's papers described the shooting as a Chicago-style drive-by. I was well pleased and polishing up my alibi when the Old Bill arrived to nick me. My dispute with Big Kenny wasn't exactly secret.

Every half-arsed grass in the manor knew there was bad blood after my stabbing. Billy Gibney was in the next cell and along from him young Bobby Dickens, a 16-year-old who had been in the back seat of the car as a passenger. Bobby was a great lad. He told the police it was him who shot the club up. They didn't believe him but what could they do? With Bobby riding shotgun, Billy told the cops he was the driver. He got 18 months in prison and served a year. We were that tight. I'd have done the time for him and he knew it. Bobby did 16 weeks out of a six-month sentence after his brief convinced the court it was high jinks that had got out of control and no one had been hurt seriously.

The cops couldn't pin anything on me. I had two watertight alibis and they already had two collars admitting everything so they had to let me go. They were gutted. I wasn't exactly celebrating because my mates were doing time for me but both Billy and Bobby were well looked after when they came out.

A few weeks after the shooting, I was minding my own business driving through Shoreditch when I got a tug from the police. A patrol car pulled me over for missing a left-turn signal. I don't know if they targeted me deliberately or whether I was just unlucky, but the two traffic cops couldn't believe their dumb luck when they realised they'd pulled Micky Glückstad over. Those mugs will get you for anything they can. As they walked round the motor, looking for something to pin on me, I thought hard trying to remember if I was carrying anything illegal. Turned out it didn't matter; the c**ts did me for drink-driving.

I'd only had a couple but it was enough to put me over the legal limit when they breathalysed me on the side of the road. The two coppers were practically dancing with joy at successfully pulling me. When they take a personal dislike to you, the police will go to any lengths to get a conviction. They don't care what for. They're only happy while you're behind bars. Still, I thought I'd probably get a slap on the wrist and a fine. Instead, West Ham magistrates took a fortune off me – £500 – and sent me to Pentonville prison for three months.

The Ville, as it is known, was a right piss-hole of a prison and every day felt like a week. Everything inside was grey. The walls, the uniforms, the food, even the colour of the smackheads. It was depressing. One of the few delights of incarceration is meeting interesting people, making new mates and meeting up with old ones. I kid you not. Prison is the underworld's version of Facebook. That's how you make friends and influence people the best, when you're locked up with them and looking down the wrong end of a long sentence.

Nothing works better than getting yourself out on the landings and making friends. It's fine to come out with a degree or some A-levels, but far better to have a bulging contacts book and plenty of work lined up.

As luck would have it, Pentonville was chronically short-staffed so we were stuck in our cells for 23 hours a day and I never met a single face. It was honestly the worst bird I ever did.

CHAPTER NINE

'A GOOD SCAM CAN BE THE SIMPLEST THING IN THE WORLD, BUT YOU'VE GOT TO KNOW WHAT YOU'RE TALKING ABOUT TO BE A PROPER CORNER MERCHANT. OR BE ABLE TO BLUFF YOUR SOCKS OFF. YOUR MARK WILL FEEL CONFIDENT IF IT SOUNDS LIKE YOU KNOW YOUR ONIONS. LIKEWISE, IF YOU START TAP DANCING LIKE MAD, ALARM BELLS WILL GO OFF AND THE PUNTER WILL SMELL A RAT. DO SOME BACKGROUND RESEARCH AND PRACTISE, PRACTISE, PRACTISE...'

THE GREAT WANSTEAD COW CON

Champagne Charlie, aka Arnie Fouste, and I were having a drink or two in the Golden Fleece pub in Manor Park. It was a lovely summer evening and the cattle were grazing peacefully on Wanstead Flats opposite, unaware of the fuss they were about to cause. Cow rustling from the area had been a booming business in past centuries and it was about to get a modern makeover.

Christ only knows who owned them – I certainly didn't – but that wasn't going to stop me flogging them when Arnie told me he'd come across two yokels who were looking to pick up some livestock on the cheap.

My first reaction was, 'No way – I know nothing about cows.' But, with his customary glass of champagne, Arnie convinced me. After all, how hard could it be? They ate grass and gave you milk. End of. And there were hundreds of them just wandering around right in front of us on Wanstead Flats. I was well known by now for being able to flog a dead horse. A living cow couldn't be much harder.

A good scam can be the simplest thing in the world, but you've got to know what you're talking about to be a proper corner merchant. Or be able to bluff your socks off. Your mark will feel confident if it sounds like you know your onions. Likewise, if you start tap dancing like mad, alarm bells will go off and the punter will smell a rat. Do some background research and practise, practise, practise. Selling stones, know the stones; selling cars, be able to pop up the bonnet at the very least; selling cows, well, know which end the milk comes out of for starters. This was before the internet and Google so I had to get up to speed the old-fashioned way. Lucky for me, we still had public libraries. Soon I could talk the hind legs off anyone about the cows of Wanstead Flats, the history of public grazing and the many fine breeds in evidence today.

Now we were waiting at the Golden Fleece for our marks to arrive. I honestly had no idea how they wound up thinking Arnie Fouste was a champion cattle dealer but I'd dressed the part in wellingtons, check shirt and a waxed jacket with a borrowed Range Rover for authenticity. Fuck knows what the bar staff thought when I rocked up looking like Farmer Giles but they were good as gold and never said a word. When Arnie's new mates arrived, it was too good to be true. So much so that I thought for a second we might be on candid camera.

Tom and Malcolm were straight out of central casting for rural types – tweed jackets, cords and wellies. They practically had straw sticking out from behind their ears. I kid you not. Arnie greeted them with a flourish. 'Hello, boys,' he said. 'This is my associate Micky – he's your man for cows.'

Malcolm and Tom were good old boys. They liked a drink and a laugh and knew a good cow when they saw one. I liked them but that wasn't going to stop me ripping them off. Let's face it, if they had any scruples they wouldn't have been buying cattle off a bloke like me, would they?

What they might have lacked in business sense they more than made up for in good humour and they had ready cash, lots of it. Coming from rural Wales in a hired van, Malcolm and Tom were obviously thrilled to be in the Smoke and it showed. They were bowled over by the reception we gave them and were soon chugging on their pints like there was no tomorrow. I had to twist their arms to get them out the door to examine the herd.

Luckily, the Wanstead cattle were well used to the attention of passers-by, having been a regular fixture in the park for donkey's years. So I grabbed the nearest cow by its ear as I'd once seen some vet do on the telly and pulled it over for my new agricultural pals to inspect.

'Now, boys, how many cows are you looking for?' I asked, my arm around the cow's neck as one of my new friends examined its teeth and feet.

Grabbing the cow by the scruff of its neck and peering into its eyes, Tom replied: 'As many of these fine beasties as you boys have got for sale.'

'In that case, you can take them all,' I said confidently. 'I'll need a seven-grand deposit, cash, and you can bring a livestock lorry tomorrow and pick them up. Let's have another drink to celebrate.'

I was keen to get the deal done as soon as and get out of this gear and back into my normal clobber. The cow had other ideas. Maybe it got the hump or maybe Tom had pinched it too hard while he was examining it, but it rocked back and thrashed its neck into my back, sending me flying.

Quick as a whippet, I was back on my feet, giving the cow a slap across the chops. With a startled moo, it retreated back towards its mates. I could see Tom and Malcolm were surprised at my technique.

'Gotta teach 'em who's boss, eh, boys?' I laughed.

'Er, yeah, I suppose so,' they replied.

The deal was done and we all celebrated with another drink. Arnie and I split the cash and left as soon as it was polite. To cut a long story short, Malcolm and Tom were nicked the next day for rustling when one of the rightful owners saw them loading his cattle into their truck. Despite their protests that they had bought the cows legally, they were taken to court.

They told the Old Bill they had bought them fair and square off a geezer down the pub. But they were taken to court in Stratford anyway. The cops never put two and two together to come up with Micky G. The magistrates laughed them right out of town. They accepted that Malcolm and Tom had been conned and gave them a slap on the wrist. The Old Bill told them to fuck off back to Wales when they tried to complain. Job done.

Despite my best efforts, the same herd was still grazing happily on Wanstead Flats for years until mad cow disease hit Britain and they were taken away for good. I was sad to see them go, really. Easiest seven grand I'd ever made and I got to keep the wellies, too. Not that I ever wore them again.

The con game is a trickster's game, and if you can keep a straight face and plausible manner you can corner anyone. If you think I've got a hundred cows to sell, I'll sit here drinking with you while my mate takes the money and goes off to seal the deal. If he doesn't come back, you get nervous and I'll buy you another drink.

If he still doesn't come back, I'll suggest maybe he's been nicked. Maybe he's clipped a car; he was drinking and he might have had a crash. Tell you what, give me your number and I'll call you later. I walk out and you've been had. That call will never come but it's all about front. If you're shaking like a leaf and bricking yourself, no one's going to buy diddly-squat off you. You've got to look and act the part. You need nerves of steel.

You can only con a greedy man, though. You can't con anyone else because they're not greedy. You go to a pub up north where they want to buy 10 grand's worth of drink. Well, they're greedy men. They want to buy stolen drink that I haven't got anyway. You've got to have a poker face. I could look straight into people's eyes and lie to them. Most of them were villains anyway, looking for a get-rich-quick scheme. I would never have a straight person over. If they're villains

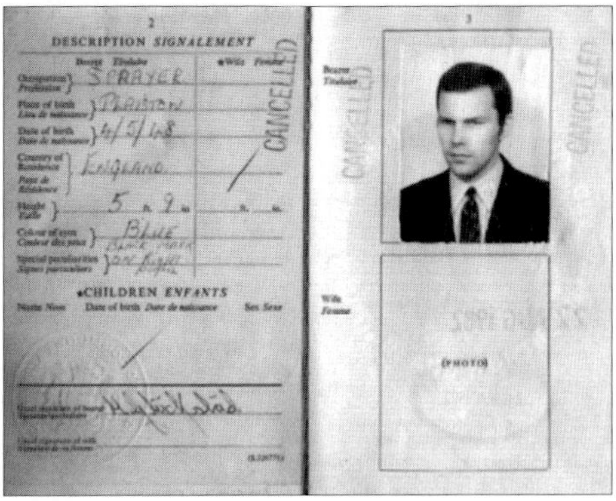

ɔove left: My beloved mum, Ivy Glückstad, during WW2 at about the ne she met my Dad. She was a real looker, and it's no surprise it was ve at first sight.

ɔove right: My dad, John Glückstad, at about the same time. I was in ison when he died and couldn't be there to say goodbye: one of the eatest regrets of my life.

low left: With my Norwegian cousins in 1960. I'm on the right-hand e. Oslo was a world away from the East End.

low right: My passport from the early-Seventies. For some reason my ɔfession is described as 'sprayer', it should have read 'player'.

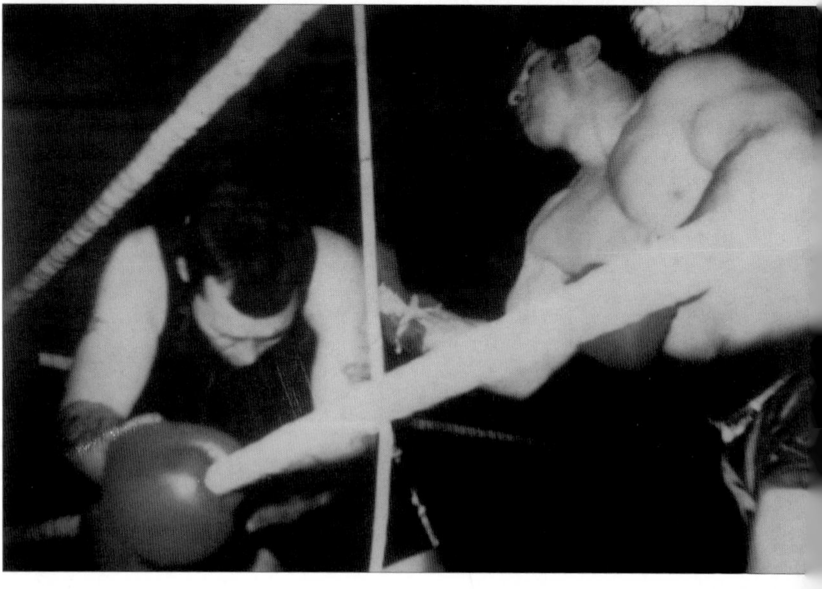

Above left: A rare shot of the Regency Club in Hackney. It was here I found myself staring down the business end of Jack 'The Hat' McVitie's sawn-off shotgun.

Above right: The Blind Beggar pub on White Chapel Road, London, is o of Britain's most famous pubs because of its connections to the Kray twi

Below: In the ring with Roy Shaw (right). To my knowledge this is the only photo in existence of our fight at Dagenham Working Men's Club i 1977. You can see how powerful Roy was but I fought him to a standsti

inally married Janet Eaton in 1978, but sadly it didn't last. We look like
y other young couple apart from my vivid ear to eye scar, the result of
attempt on my life.

Above: Billy, Eileen, Alan and Brenda in the early-Seventies. Billy was a real hard-nut and introduced me to the Kray twins. Alan backed me to the tune of two grand so I could fight Roy Shaw.

Below: Drinking in the Seventies at the Green Gate club, Stratford. My good friend, Mike Tucker (right), was governor there for a time. Most of my unofficial fights were in bars or pub car parks.

ged 28 in 1976. I fancied myself as a playboy and a bit of a stud.

Above: Not all the fighting took place in pubs and car parks. Fighting heavyweight Terry Sharp (left) at Cinatra's nightclub in Croydon in 1976 In the foreground is the legendary Nosher Powell, who refereed many of the most famous official fights of the era.

Below right: With my only son Michael in 1980. Sadly, we're now estranged

Below left: Arnie Fouste, AKA 'Champagne Charlie' (left), and our pal Lenny Green (centre). I have no idea where I got the sheepskin jacket from – probably off the back of a lorry.

bove: Danny Woollard and me. He is one of my oldest pals. We've been
rough thick and thin together, and he's always had my back.

elow: Here I am with the next generation of hard men, Billy Boy Yates,
n of the legendary fighter and face Lew Yates. His tattoos make mine
ok tame.

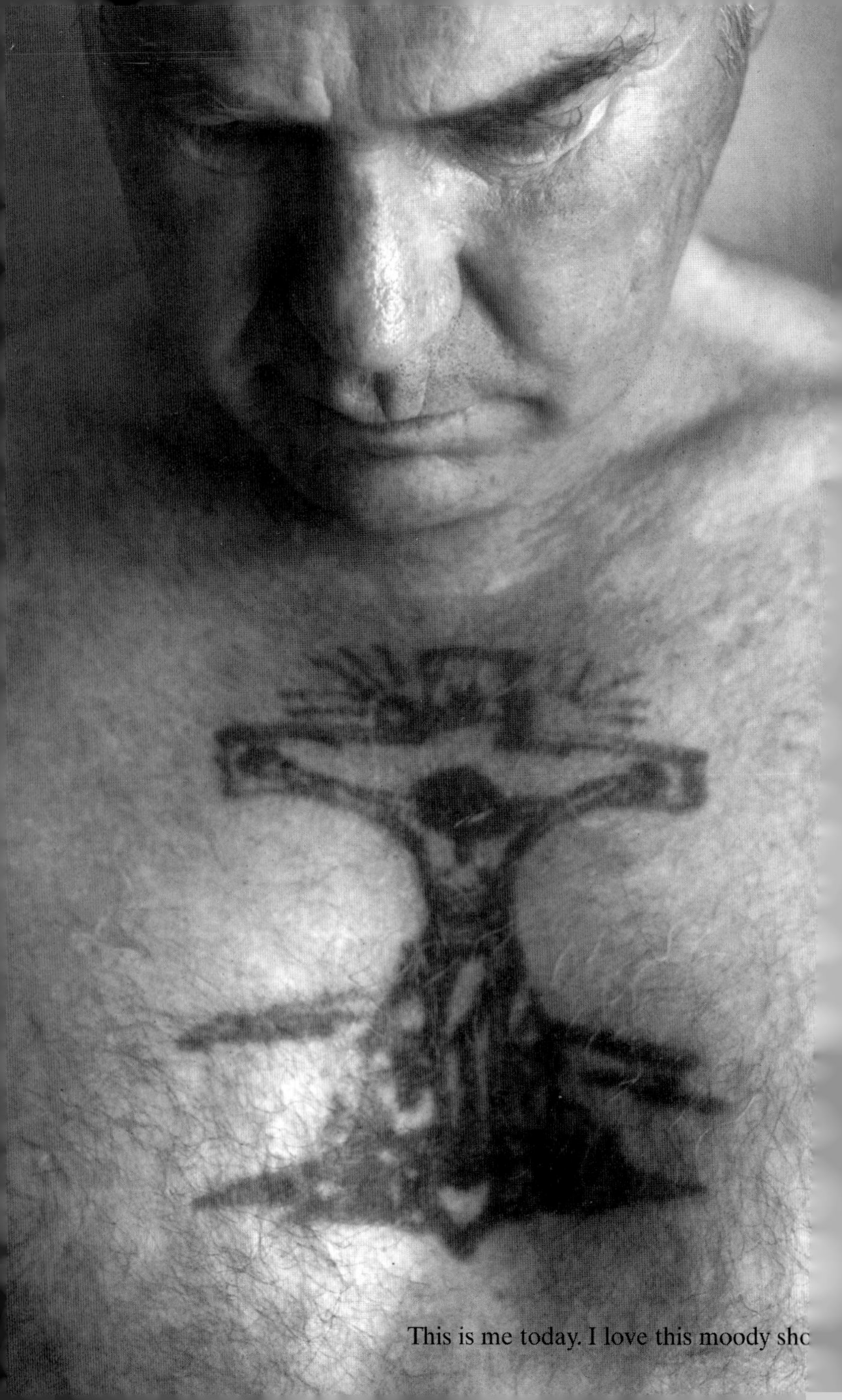

This is me today. I love this moody sho

they've got their money their way and I've got it my way. I've been up north a lot of times selling non-existent dodgy goods. But it wasn't just flogging stuff. There was good money to be made all over the shop.

One of my weirdest experiences came when I was briefly employed as a driving instructor. Maybe employed is pushing it. I was having breakfast in Pellicci's café in Bethnal Green when Arnie Fouste rocked up with a big smile on his face.

'Mick, I'm knocking about with a brass,' he said.

'Morning, Arnie. So what?' I replied.

'So she's taking her driving test at Barking test centre next week,' he continued. 'I told her I knew an examiner there and for £500 I would get him to guarantee she would pass. She agreed but she'll only pay the examiner on completion of the test. I don't know any examiners – I was going to take her money and disappear.'

'OK,' I said, 'what's the date and time of her test?'

'Next Wednesday at 10.45am.'

'OK, you bring her to meet me at 10.15am and walk in with her. Make sure she brings the money in an envelope.'

So, the next Wednesday at 10am I was waiting in the Barking test centre wearing a pair of glasses I'd borrowed, a smart jacket, shirt and tie and carrying an official-looking clipboard (nothing gives people confidence in your official status as much as a clipboard). There were four or five punters waiting to take their tests so I dawdled by the noticeboards waiting for Arnie. Bang on time he arrived with his mark. She was a nice-looking blonde and I introduced myself, clipboard under my arm.

'Miss Wilson?'

'Yes.'

'Good morning. I'm Mr King, your examiner for today. Shall we go?'

Outside the test centre, I asked her, 'Right, Miss Wilson, where did you park?'

'Over there,' she replied, pointing to a smart blue Escort.

'Lovely,' I said, then to Arnie: 'We won't need you, sir. Perhaps you'd like to wait in that café along the road. We'll be along in about half an hour.'

We drove off down the road until I spotted a side street and asked her to pull over. She was a terrible driver and, frankly, I was worried she might hit something and then I'd be in real trouble.

'Park here, Miss Wilson,' I told her. 'Now, have you got something for me, an envelope?'

'Yes, Mr King, here it is,' she said eagerly.

I opened the brown envelope, checked the money and pocketed it. Now I thought I'd have some fun with her.

'You're an awful driver,' I told her. 'You need to really take it easy or I'll lose my job. You really aren't qualified to drive. You need a hell of a lot more practice.'

Flustered now, she replied: 'I'm driving badly because my nerves have got the better of me.'

'Well, that may be true, but you'll need to be careful. Obviously don't tell anyone about our little deal.'

'Of course not,' she fluttered.

It was about 20 minutes later now so I asked her to turn us round and head back to the test centre. She nearly crashed three or four times and my knuckles were white from gripping the sides of my seat by the time she pulled back into her spot on the forecourt of the test centre.

'Now, Miss Wilson, it's my pleasure to tell you you've passed your driving test,' I said. 'You wait here and I'll go into the centre to fill in the appropriate forms and get your pass certificate. If you join your friend in the café, I'll bring them down to you.'

She couldn't have been more thrilled. 'Thank you, Mr King,' she said.

I nipped into the centre and gave it a couple of minutes before slipping out a side door and jumping in my own car. Miss Wilson was nowhere to be seen as I sped away. I met Arnie later and we split the £500. But he couldn't resist winding Miss Wilson up and called her a couple of days later.

'You bastard,' she spat down the phone. 'I've got two minders working for me and we know that your Mr King is actually Micky Glückstad. They know where he drinks and they're going to kill him.'

Arnie tipped me off so I called her to try to sort things out.

'Hello, Miss Wilson. Mr King here.'

She screamed down the phone: 'You bastard, you're dead.'

'Am I?' I replied. 'Well, you tell your fucking minders I'm looking for them now and if I catch them they're dead. So we're even.'

I put the phone down and thought no more of it. Soon after, Danny Woollard had a call from an old pal. Angelo Hayman was a very tidy half-Maltese hard man with a formidable reputation for dishing out punishment, but a good bloke too.

'Danny, you're friendly with Micky Glückstad, aren't you?' he asked.

'Yes, I am,' Danny told him.

'Can we meet with him tomorrow night at your club? There's no bother, we just need to sort something out.'

'No problem, Angelo. I'll get Micky along.'

Danny phoned and the next night we met at Danny's place, the Hathaway Club at Manor Park. Angelo turned up with Royston 'Little Legs' Smith, a dwarf who'd once worked for the Krays and a very hard little man. They were a fearsome pair but Danny knew Angelo and trusted him and I trusted Danny with my life.

About 15 minutes later I rocked up and they told their story.

'Mick,' said Angelo, 'Roy's been minding a brothel and the woman that runs it told him she wants someone to shoot you. I went and saw her and told her it was £4,000 – £2,000 upfront and another £2,000 when the job's done.

'She didn't know me from Adam and we've split the cash. Now I've disappeared and Roy's told her I've been nicked and sent to prison. We just wanted to let you know you didn't need to watch your back. I've heard you're looking for us so I just wanted to let you know the score. No hard feelings.'

'None at all, Angelo, Roy,' I replied, laughing. 'Nice to know I'm not the only one in the cornering game. Good job, boys.'

* * *

One of my greatest moments in prison was conning a screw out of £10,000. I'll say that again: I was inside and I managed to con one of the prison guards out of 10 grand. It was a very sweet moment.

This guy was a proper muppet. He'd read all the gangland books about the Krays and the old East End and he was enamoured. It went one of two ways with screws; usually they hated you and everything they thought you stood for. But some secretly wanted to be like you. They should've seen banged-up lags as the ultimate warning but they didn't. They thought, if these guys can make easy money through crime, why not me too? Silly sods.

This one bloke was properly thick. I have no idea how he became a prison officer but he was star struck with some of the cons. He was always asking me about Reg and Ronnie Kray, the Richardsons, Jack McVitie. I told him, truthfully, that I knew them all and shared some of the stories from back in the day. As we became friendlier, he admitted he wanted to make a big chunk of money and asked if I could help him. Well, naturally, advice doesn't come cheap so I strung him along for a bit. Got some favours, some cushy assignments and the like.

Then we sat down and I said one word: 'drugs'. That was how he could make a killing. Now, I'd never touched drugs and never dealt them. Hated them in fact. I'd seen some close friends lose everything to cocaine and heroin. I wasn't letting on though, and I told my boy that if he could put up £10,000 I could turn it into £40,000 in a weekend by investing in a drug buy.

His eyes were bulging out of his head. 'Do you mean that, Micky? And no risk to me?'

What a sucker. I had no intention of getting mixed up in a drugs deal from behind bars but I also knew he wouldn't want to kick up a stink if it went pear-shaped. So I smiled and shafted him.

On my next weekend home visit we met in a pub away from the prison.

He'd brought the cash in a small black briefcase like something out of *The Godfather*. Like I said, he was in love with the glamour of the underworld.

'This is my life savings, Micky,' he told me. 'Please make sure you don't lose it.'

'No problem, mate,' I lied. 'It's in safe hands. I know these people. We can trust them. It's easy money.'

He didn't even ask what was in it for me. I almost felt sorry for him. As I said, he wasn't the sharpest knife in the drawer. Even the other screws used to call him 'Sarnie' because he was one sandwich short of a full picnic. But now the con was on and it gave me a proper buzz.

The money never went near any drugs, unless you count the empty paracetamol packet under my mum's bed where I stashed the dosh until I could dispose of it properly. I went home and enjoyed my weekend.

Back in prison on Monday, Sarnie could hardly contain himself. 'All right, Micky, how did it go then?' he boomed down the landing.

'Mate, keep it down; you'll get us all nicked,' I warned him.

'Sorry, Micky. What's the news?' he whispered.

'All good. Money's delivered, deal's on for this weekend. I'll pick up your loot the next time I'm on weekend release.'

The look on his face was priceless. I could see him mentally sizing up the new car he was going to buy. Honestly, anyone who thinks they can make 40 big ones overnight for nothing is having a laugh.

A couple of weeks went by and Sarnie started to get a bit jumpy about his money. After my next weekend release, I decided it was time to put him out of his misery.

'Sorry, mate, they've all been nicked. The cops were waiting at the buy and they were all rolled up.'

'What about my money, my savings?' he stammered.

'All gone, mate. I'm sorry but that's how it is. The cops will be trying to find the banker but my boys are good. They won't grass on us.'

His expression went from horror to anger to fear in seconds. Poor bugger. Next thing he was thanking me for protecting him. It was like taking candy from a baby. I never saw him again. He went off on sick leave that afternoon and never came back. That was a nice bit of business. If I hadn't taken his money, he'd only have gone and done something stupid and got himself into real trouble.

Aside from the cows, and prison officers, I was never that lucky with animals. One time, Billy Gibney asked me to come with him to Tilbury to collect some money a bloke owed him. We motored down to Tilbury docks to the fellow's yard but he didn't want to pay Billy. He had two huge Alsatians chained up and he clearly believed they would scare us away. Billy was terrified of dogs and sweating with fear but I couldn't have cared less.

'Get out of my yard. You can whistle for your money,' the bloke told Billy.

With that, he released the first dog, which went for Billy, jaws gaping. I stepped straight in and, as the dog leapt for Bill's throat, punched it straight in the ribs in mid-air. There was a cracking sound and a whimper and the dog went flying.

Then Bill shouted, 'Look out, Mick.'

The other dog was off its chain and coming at me howling.

As it leapt at me, snarling, I grabbed it by the throat with one hand and punched it under the ribs with the other. Then, after throwing it to the ground, I kicked and punched it until it was whimpering and crying like its mate.

Don't get me wrong, I don't like hurting animals but I had no choice. These were properly vicious dogs bred for one purpose: ripping the throat out of anyone who got on their owner's wick. They weren't there for petting purposes for sure. Proper Hound of the Baskervilles-type mutts.

'Please can we have our money now,' I asked Billy's mate politely.

The fellow took one look at his two dogs and paid up immediately.

'Micky,' said Billy, 'if I hadn't seen that with my own eyes I don't think I'd have believed it.'

I laughed. 'Don't tell anyone, Bill. Or the people who think I'm mad will really start to believe it.'

As [illegible] I grabbed [illegible] by the throat with one hand and [illegible] the other. [illegible] I kicked [illegible] [illegible] like [illegible]

[illegible]

[illegible]

[illegible] don't think I'd have believed it.'

[illegible]

CHAPTER TEN

'HE LOOKED FINISHED BUT WAS FIGHTING ON. HE WAS LUNGING AT ME LIKE A WOUNDED BULL, ROARING IN FRUSTRATION AS I DUCKED AWAY, LETTING HIM WEAR HIMSELF DOWN. EACH TIME, I STEPPED BACK AND SHOOK THE SWEAT OUT OF MY EYES. FINALLY, AS HE LAUNCHED HIMSELF AT ME, I SAW MY OPENING, SIDESTEPPED, AND SMASHED HIM IN THE KIDNEYS WITH BOTH FISTS BALLED TOGETHER. HE MUST'VE BEEN IN AGONY – I DON'T DOUBT HE WAS PISSING BLOOD LATER...'

KING OF THE GYPSIES

Many men have claimed the title King of the Gypsies – an accolade marking them as the best bare-knuckle fighter in the travelling community – but none of them carries the honour for long. There is always a young pretender to the throne waiting in the wings. The gypsy community loves the barbarity of a bare-knuckle bout like no other. Even in today's politically correct age, bare-knuckle or full-contact fighting continues to thrive underground in various forms. Despite the best efforts of the authorities, as long as men have an ego and some bollocks, there will always be contests in empty factories, car parks and fairground fields.

I fought numerous gypsies during my career, including Donny Adams in front of the Krays at Barnet Horse Fair, but one bout stands out to this day. When I fought the then Gypsy King Levi Silks to a standstill. It was one of the hardest fights of my life. Silks was no novice and had a punch like the kick of a mule, as the gypsies like to say, as well as a fearsome reputation as a mauler that was borne out by his scarred hands, broken nose and lumpy, torn ears like an alley cat.

Thousands, maybe even tens of thousands, of pounds changed hands over the course of our fight. People said we were evenly matched but there would be no points decision; this fight would go the distance until one of us was vanquished.

As usual, I'd been trying hard to keep out of trouble. Danny Woollard had a nice little earner going, buying up empty beer barrels and melting them down for their aluminium content. It was honest too, as far as we were concerned. Pub landlords looking for some readies would flog the barrels to us then tell the breweries they'd been stolen. Danny had a lorry and we'd go round the pubs and clubs of the East End picking up barrels for smelting.

One day Danny and I were at a club in Barking. We'd paid for 100 barrels at £3 each from the bar manager and had loaded them up in the yard behind the club when a thickset ginger bloke came up to us oozing attitude.

'Where are you going?' he asked.

'What's it got to do with you?' I replied.

So the ginger bloke got right in my face and snarled: 'Are you fucking deaf? What are you doing with my barrels?'

I told him we'd paid for them fair and square but he didn't feel like negotiating.

'Now you've got to pay me,' he replied, 'or else you ain't leaving my yard.'

Just then two other blokes walked up, pulling the heavy iron gates shut behind them.

Danny, who was sitting in the driver's seat of the lorry, ready to roll, looked over at me and winked. Leaning out of the cab window, he told Ginger: 'All right, mate. We'll pay you for them. We don't want any trouble.'

The arrogant fucker smiled: 'That's more like it, girls.'

Danny turned the key and the motor roared to life. Before Ginger could blink, he'd floored the pedal and smashed through the gates, leaving them a twisted pile of scrap and running down one of the two heavies. Now it was two on two and Ginger and his remaining mate came storming over.

Danny pulled over, jumped out of the cab with a spanner,

and smashed Ginger's mate across the nose. He went down straight away, screaming blue murder. I grabbed Ginger by the scruff of his neck and whacked him across the mouth. He was a big bloke and clearly fancied himself. Twisting out of my grip, he caught me a glancing blow off my forehead. Danny saw me and started in.

'Keep out of this, Danny. It's one on one,' I screamed.

At first, Ginger gave as good as he got, to be fair. But this fight was only going to end one way – with Ginger on his arse and regretting having got up that morning. I knocked him down five times and, on the fifth, he stayed down, puking his guts up in the gutter. I was bleeding heavily from a cut above my left eye but otherwise unhurt. With that, we jumped in the lorry and drove off.

Sometime afterwards, the same bloke was brutally murdered. I doubt anyone mourned him. He had a horrible reputation as a bully, a real nasty character.

Sadly, Danny's furnace blew up soon after so that put paid to our smelting scam, but it had been nice money while it lasted. Danny branched out into the scrap metal business but that was too much like hard work for me, so, in the words of Charles Dickens' Mr Micawber, a hero of mine, I was again 'waiting for something to turn up'.

But turn up it did, and quicker than I had anticipated. The 'something' before me was Levi Silks, who was to be one of the most memorable opponents of my life.

Silks lived in a trailer at a scrapyard in Dagenham, next to the aptly named Three Travellers public house. Somehow he'd got wind of my reputation for never backing down from a fight and reckoned I'd be an easy win. A match was arranged and, on the day, thousands of spectators had piled on to the Lees Common in Yalding, a small village outside Maidstone in Kent, where our clash was to take place. There are many links between the East End and the travelling community and both were well represented. Fuck knows what the locals made of it but it was one of the great fights and the police never got wind until it was over.

As ever, Danny and Billy Gibney were my corner men: watching my back, looking after the money and keeping an eye on the referee to ensure a fair fight. I was well fancied to win among the East Enders who knew me but plenty were hedging their bets with money on the Gypsy King too.

The rules were simple: three-minute rounds with a 30-second break in between until one of us went down or couldn't continue. Each of us would have a second and, if we were knocked out and could be revived for the next round, the fight would continue. It would only stop when one of us was too badly injured to carry on. We wore no gloves and expected no mercy from our opponent. Neither would we offer any. It was the original unlicensed sport of strength at its most brutal. Men have been fighting since they came out of their caves and I've no doubt they'll be at it even when we're all living in space ships. I'm happy to have played my part in history.

For once I trained hard. I laid off the booze for a few weeks and found time for some bag work in a local gym. I needed the money and couldn't afford to blow this fight like a mug through not having enough puff. Wherever I went, people talked to me about my chances in the forthcoming bout.

Unlicensed boxing peaked in popularity in the seventies. There were weekly fights and the big names had their own following. We were like footballers with our working-class fan base – idolised and admired, if not as well paid. Like football, money took over the sport and professionalised it. Many would say ruined it too, but, as I say, it'll always be there in its most primal form bubbling away below the surface whether blokes are fighting for pride or a purse or for the sheer hell of it.

All these thoughts were flooding my mind as I sat in the back of Billy's car on the way to the fight. It was a light spring day and the first thing I noticed at the Lees was how quiet it was despite the big crowds. Some entrepreneurial hawkers had set out their stalls selling booze and burgers around the edge of the common and whole families had arrived to enjoy the warm weather and a day out in the country with a bit of mindless violence thrown in. But amid the carnival atmosphere, and the dozens of little kids dashing about and shouting to their parents with excitement, there was an intense air of expectation. People really did want to see if we had what it took to tear each other apart. I couldn't speak for Silks but I knew I was ready.

The fight took place on a raised wooden platform, about as professionally done as you'd ever expect for a bare-knuckle bout. I limbered up by stretching my arms, rolling my head around and jogging on the spot. I was never one for shadow-boxing, as technique was not my strongest point. If I could be fast and resourceful I knew I had it in me to beat Silks. By now the crowd was whipping itself up into a frenzy and I could hear the shouts for my opponent to tear me apart.

The ref pulled us together in the centre of the ring and held our arms up together as he introduced us to the crowd. 'Give it up for Micky Glückstad from the East End. The man who beat Roy Shaw.' There was an enormous cheer. But it was immediately overshadowed by Silks' reception – everyone going wild for this man who lived humbly in a caravan surrounded by piles of rusting cars, ancient washing machines and old bathtubs. The ref grabbed us again. 'Now, gentlemen,' he said, 'touch hands then it's up to you.'

As the bell went, I felt an enormous surge of energy pulsing through my body. Silks danced towards me, hyping the crowd and performing some fancy footwork to draw me in. I didn't give a fuck. I stood still, waiting for him to come at me, and come at me he did, darting in to flick his fists at my head.

It must've looked clever to the watching mob because they screamed with delight, but he was toying with me and I didn't like it one bit. Ignoring his fists, I thundered into him, swinging my arms and catching him on the chin. The crowd gasped as he pulled back, recovering quickly, but I was at him again, and again. I wasn't going to let up the pressure. I wanted to pull his arms off and use them to batter him to death, I was so wound up on the adrenalin.

The gypsy was the heavier and bigger man, but I was faster and was hurting him. We danced backwards and forwards for five full rounds, chasing each other round the ring and puffing and panting like thirsty bulldogs on a hot day.

By round six, Silks looked finished but was fighting on. He was lunging at me like a wounded bull, roaring in frustration as I ducked away, letting him wear himself down. Each time, I stepped back and shook the sweat out of my eyes. Finally, as he launched himself at me, I saw my opening, sidestepped, and smashed him in the kidneys with both fists balled together. He must've been in agony – I don't doubt he was pissing blood later – but he pulled himself to his feet and conceded the fight like a proper man, raising his hands in appreciation.

There had been little finesse and no KO and I was worried the crowd was going to go berserk, but Levi was a hugely popular fighter and his gracious defeat was met with a well-natured cheer. We shook hands and hugged – there was no malice. It had been a fair fight and I had won. Sadly, some years later, I learned that Silks had died of cancer, an evil disease that doesn't discriminate between taking the lives of kings or paupers. Well, Levi Silks was a true king and a true gentleman.

CHAPTER ELEVEN

'ALL I HEARD WAS A SPLASH AND THEN I REALISED SHE'D GONE OVER THE SIDE INTO THE THAMES. SHE COULDN'T SWIM AND WAS BEING DRAGGED UNDER BY THE CURRENTS IN THE DARK, COLD WATER. I DIVED IN AFTER HER. I WAS A POWERFUL SWIMMER, BUT THE CURRENT WAS TOO STRONG AND I NEVER REACHED HER IN TIME. SHE DIDN'T CRY OUT ONCE. JUST SLIPPED AWAY...'

THAMES TRAGEDY

Some jobs are best avoided, no matter how juicy they sound. You just have a gut feeling that something ain't right. If only I'd listened to my instincts when I bumped into a geezer I knew named Ernie while having a quiet drink in Bow one afternoon. Ernie was a quiet bloke, a long-distance lorry driver who wouldn't say boo to a goose and had never been in trouble with the law.

Today he was buzzing. A friend had tipped him off about a stash of electrical goods in a warehouse in Woodgrange Road, Forest Gate, and suddenly he was being Billy Big Bollocks about turning it over. Given his inexperience, I should have heard alarm bells and avoided the job like the plague, but it sounded like easy meat. A skylight gave access to the warehouse and there was no guard or alarm. All we needed was a van and some luck. Well, we got the van.

The following Saturday, Ernie was getaway driver and lookout in an alley round the back while I shimmied up a drainpipe, climbed across the roof and levered open the skylight. As promised, it came up easily and there was no alarm. I lowered myself through the gap and down into the warehouse. It was an Aladdin's cave of televisions and radios, all brand new and in their boxes.

Christ, I thought. We should've brought a bigger lorry.

With that, I opened the doors and Ernie scampered in. He could hardly contain his excitement and I had to warn him to calm down. We were looking at a serious haul, even if we only managed to cart away half the goods. It was Christmas come early for 15 minutes as we loaded up the van. Then Christmas got cancelled. I was balancing a couple of tellies on the back of the van, trying to make room to squeeze them in, when there was a shout and Ernie appeared from the front collared by two huge policemen, one of whom had him by the scruff of the neck. I looked round but there was no point making a run for it.

We were stuffed, caught red-handed. Later I learned we'd been set up and ambushed. The Flying Squad had been under pressure to take a few scalps and dangled the juicy target as bait. They must've been delighted when two gormless fuckers like us took it lock, stock and barrel.

We appeared before Stratford magistrates the next day and were remanded to Brixton prison. Two weeks later, we were hauled in front of the judge at Snaresbrook Crown Court. I told the judge the plan was mine and I'd talked Ernie, with his lack of previous, into helping. It didn't wash and the old buzzard gave us both a year. Given his clean record, Ernie was sent to Ford Open Prison, a Category D establishment in West Sussex. The judge looked at my juvenile and borstal record and sent me to Camp Hill Barracks, a grim Cat. C prison on the Isle of Wight for first-time adult offenders. Camp Hill had been built in 1912 using prison labour from nearby Parkhurst prison and opened by Winston Churchill himself. I doubt anyone had given the place a lick of paint during the intervening years. It was crowded and nasty and the regime was based on an army boot camp.

We were woken at 6am for compulsory physical training in

the yard in rain, snow or shine. All the prisoners wore heavy boots and army-style garters along with the rough serge uniforms and the screws were as hard as the blocks of granite used to construct the towering black walls. It was miserable and I was allocated to the toughest work party in the prison. Every day we were marched double quick into an adjoining field where we were ordered to dig five-foot-square holes, then fill them in again. It was a back-breaking and totally pointless punishment and the screws constantly goaded us. That was fine; I could take it. I enjoyed being outside and could feel myself getting fitter by the day. There was just one small problem: a couple of real bullies in the work party. They loved making life difficult for the weaker prisoners, shoving earth into their holes and generally pushing them about. It was only a matter of time before they tried it on with me.

When the moment came I was ready. After two days, one of them asked me: 'What are you looking at?'

I could see the screw at the end of the field shouting at another prisoner. I didn't even answer, swinging my shovel in an arc from behind and catching bully one on the back of his head. He folded like a wet newspaper and went head first into his half-dug hole. Before bully number two could raise a squeak, I'd clobbered him the same way. He went down in a heap without a sound. Both of them were blotto. It had taken just seconds.

I carried on working, as the two thugs were stretchered away covered in mud and bleeding. I told the screw they had been fighting among themselves. I knew he didn't believe me but no one would grass and he hadn't seen a thing. When they came back from the Parkhurst hospital wing a week later, neither said a single word. They never picked on anyone again either. That was the first of a few fights inside Camp Hill but I was still young and fast and kept on my toes and was never beaten.

That same month, October 1969, a huge riot broke out in Parkhurst when 'Mad' Frankie Fraser and his fellow cons tried to take over the prison. Someone had squealed to the governor but, rather than close down the protest by keeping the inmates locked up, the authorities bussed in extra screws in riot gear. When trouble kicked off, they went in mob-handed, battering everyone in sight. Frankie, a member of the notorious Richardson gang who ultimately spent 42 years of his life in at least 20 different prisons, ended up in hospital for six weeks recovering from the hiding before being sent to Wandsworth to complete his sentence. Three of his pals, all serving long sentences, ended up in Camp Hill as the alleged troublemakers were weeded out. They told me it was the hardest prison they'd done time in.

I kept my head down from then on and was out after eight months. Crossing the Solent on the ferry back to England was the best feeling. I was stronger and fitter than I'd ever been and, what was more, there was a gorgeous blonde sitting opposite. We got talking. She was 21, from East London, beautiful, and called Maureen Wright. She had been visiting a relative on the Isle of Wight and I spent the entire train journey back to London chatting her up. I'd always fancied myself as a bit of a playboy but I fell hard for Maureen. She was great company – vivacious, funny and looked terrific. I thought we made a good couple and took her everywhere.

But I was back inside prison within months after being caught up in a robbery. For once, I was innocent. On the way back from having a cuppa with Arnie Fouste and Billy Gibney, I'd been driving past Durning Hall community centre in Forest Gate when I recognised a tall blonde with legs up to her armpits having a row with three blokes. The statuesque young lady might have looked the biz, but she was actually a bloke called Lee, a friend of Gibney's who he'd met inside while doing time for robbery. Pulling over, I called out and Lee wasted no time in jumping into the car and urging me to drive off, her short skirt riding up over what were, admittedly, a perfect pair of pins for a bloke.

She was flustered. It turned out someone had robbed the safe at Durning Hall and the three blokes had accused Lee of being involved. Ever the gentleman, I offered to drop her home, but before we got half a mile down the road a police car was screaming up behind us with its siren blaring and lights blazing. I should've pulled over there and then, but I really hated the police by now. They'd only try to stitch me up for the robbery. Stupidly, I thought I could get away. I floored the accelerator and shot off down the road doing about 70mph with Lee screaming beside me.

Almost inevitably, we were arrested. But not before I'd managed to smash through a row of bollards and rammed an oncoming police car on the Romford Road, battering four coppers, one of whom ended up in hospital, before they finally overpowered me. Thinking on my feet when it came to court, I told the judge my cup of tea had been spiked with an acid-impregnated sugar lump and my behaviour the result of terrifying hallucinations. Drugs like LSD were still seen as the preserve of musicians and hippies and the court listened rapt as I spun a tale worthy of the greatest science fiction. I'd been running from monsters with glowing heads, webbed feet and scales, your honour. What I now knew to be a police car had appeared as a huge Viking ship carrying more terrifying creatures, including the four coppers I'd battered. Lee told the court she suffered from amnesia and couldn't remember anything.

In reality I'd never touched drugs, as far as I knew, but my testimony muddied the waters nicely and the case made the national papers the next day: 'Man fights LSD monsters'. I got off on the trumped-up robbery charges but got 18 months for dangerous driving and fighting the police – a result, given I'd been charged with grievous bodily harm and actual bodily harm four times apiece.

My reputation as a hard nut was getting around the prison system as I arrived at Wandsworth to begin my sentence and the screws gave me a tough time from day one. I was up before the governor almost weekly for fighting and giving lip to the guards and felt myself being dragged into the darker reaches of Britain's creaking Victorian criminal justice system.

Then I got my 'Dear John'. If I had been struggling before, Maureen's letter sent me spiralling into the depths of depression and despair.

'Dear Micky,' she wrote, 'this is the most difficult letter of my life…'

I'd been dumped. The letter had arrived unannounced and unwanted in the weekly prisoners' postbag. Not only had she ended our relationship, she was leaving me to marry a copper and move to Wolverhampton. Her rejection, while I was behind bars and depressed as hell, nearly sent me over the edge. I could hardly believe it; dumped for a pig? My frustration and rage overcame me and, blood boiling with fury, I smashed up my cell then fought the guards when they came to subdue me.

When I'd recovered from the beating, I wrote back. My letter to Maureen was just one line long, but its contents would haunt me for years to come. It said simply: 'You won't live to see your twenty-second birthday.' I would have plenty of opportunities later to regret those nine words, scrawled in black biro on prison-issue paper when I was at my lowest ebb and reeling from her snub.

The prison doctor had been monitoring my behaviour. I had become an inveterate troublemaker and he wanted me sectioned under the Mental Health Act and out of Wandsworth for good. If he had his way, I'd never get out. Conspiring with the governor, he was planning to have me moved to Rampton high-security hospital in Nottinghamshire, where they could throw away the key for all he cared. For once I was scared. I wasn't insane. I was angry after being stitched up by the police and dumped by my girlfriend and the system was trying to break me. In the light of my protests, a leading psychiatrist was brought in from Harley Street to assess me. We met in the governor's office with two guards standing by in case I got violent.

For some reason a red snooker ball was sat on the desk in front of me.

'Can you peel that orange, Glückstad?' asked the psychiatrist.

He was having a laugh, wasn't he?

Keeping a straight face, I replied: 'I'll eat it if you can peel it, sir. But you might have trouble. It looks a bit tough to me.'

He laughed and we talked for an hour. He was a decent man and, at the end, he told me: 'You are no more insane than I am, Glückstad. There's plenty in here who are far worse than you. I'm not recommending you be moved to Rampton.'

Thank fuck for that. I'd had enough of padded cells and knockout injections in borstal and I didn't want to revisit *One Flew Over the Cuckoo's Nest*.

The governor and prison doctor were furious. They were stuck with me now and dumped me in the lifers' wing in revenge. Ordinarily, you had to be serving 10 years or more to be stuck on D Wing at Wandsworth. I was midway through a poxy 18-month stretch but they made a special exception for me.

Something had clicked in my head and I started to come out of my gloom. I began writing to my family and friends again – I'd stopped after Maureen had dumped me – and tried to adapt better to life inside. At least on the lifers' wing I had a cell to myself. They were like small railway arches, about 12 feet by 8 feet, and we were only allowed out for a couple of hours a day. I made up for it by jogging on the spot for hours on end, shadow-boxing and lifting my bed for exercise.

I tried to remember everyone I'd ever met, everywhere I'd ever been, everything I'd ever done, to try to keep my mind in shape. I still got into a few fights but only one in particular comes to mind.

My rival, who was doing 15 years for killing his wife, was

known as the Sergeant because he'd been an NCO in the army. He was the hardest bloke I'd ever met up till then, let alone fought. He must've been 40-odd and only about five feet eight but wiry, with not an ounce of fat on his body. He was a red band prisoner, which meant he was trusted with certain privileges and had access to the landings to mop them, and I made the mistake of taking the piss.

He floored me before I could throw a single punch as we went toe to toe. I later found out he was an expert in unarmed combat and a former karate champion. After five minutes, my entire body hurt. He destroyed me but it was fair and square so there were no hard feelings on either side. That was one beating I was happy to get. It knocked some sense into me.

At the time the Angry Brigade, a bunch of muddled left-wing revolutionaries, was blowing up banks, embassies and the homes of Conservative MPs in a protest against the Vietnam War and capitalism. They'd planted at least 25 bombs before being nicked. Two cells down from me was Jake Prescott, a working-class Scottish lad who'd been given 15 years for his role in the bombings. Later he said he was the only one who was angry and his co-conspirators, a bunch of middle-class art student dropouts, were 'more like the Slightly Cross Brigade'. He was a nice bloke and we talked a lot about our working-class roots. He'd been a petty criminal like me before becoming a terrorist. The screws gave him a lot of aggro because he was seen as an enemy of the state. It got worse for all of us when one of the screws was shot in the legs outside the prison in March 1972.

The Angry Brigade claimed responsibility and the screws gave all of us on the lifers' wing a beating as revenge for the attack. Wandsworth in the seventies was a mess – there were at least two suicides during my time inside.

While inside I had the pleasure of meeting and getting to know one of the most feared men in the prison system. 'Mad' Frankie Fraser had been transferred to Wandsworth for his role in the notorious Parkhurst riot while I was at neighbouring Camp Hill and we spent a lot of time talking. He was only a little fellow, and rarely talked about his work on behalf of the Richardsons, but he was feared nonetheless. If you were stupid enough to take Frankie on, you'd better be prepared to go the whole way and kill him because he would never forgive or forget you. One day you'd wake up with a knife at your throat and that would be it. He was a truly ruthless man. But if you showed respect he was good as gold. Not that the governor would have agreed. Frankie was always trying to start riots and stir up trouble behind bars. Because of this he was doubtful about his chances of being released.

'They don't like me, Mick,' he'd say, 'and I fucking hate them. I just can't find it in me to forgive them for locking me up.'

There was a lot of bad blood, but most of the cons looked up to Frankie as a leader. The problem was, he was stirring trouble over nothing. Demanding better fish or more chips with our meals.

I suppose it was his way of fighting the system and keeping his sanity. All respect to him for that. Every man deals with prison in his own way, and driving the governor mad was Frankie's. With just seven weeks left of my sentence I got caught up in one of Frankie's sit-ins in protest at something or other.

I'd been walking in the yard with Frankie and Arthur Hosein, who, along with his brother Nizamodeen, had been jailed for the kidnapping of Muriel McKay, the wife of one of media baron Rupert Murdoch's lieutenants, in the belief she was the wife of the Australian owner of the *News of the World* and the *Sun*.

She had been held for ransom and later killed. The brothers, both of whom I served time with at different points, used to claim they had cut her body up and fed it to the pigs because she was never found, dead or alive. We were chatting when, suddenly, Frankie announced his latest sit-in. About half the cons disappeared immediately, including Arthur, the fucking chickens. Because I was with Frankie, I thought I'd better sit down too. It wouldn't do to leave him looking like a mug, no matter how damaging it might be to my own chances of getting out.

Given events at other jails, the governor wasn't in the mood to tolerate any insubordination, or let events escalate out of control as they had at Parkhurst two years earlier. Fifty extra screws were shipped in immediately to crack heads, and Frankie's latest insurrection was over before it had begun when the riot squad charged the yard mob-handed and tooled up with batons and shields.

The ringleaders were beaten savagely and dragged to the punishment block to cool off. Later, Frankie, myself and three other inmates were taken before the governor to explain our actions. I kept quiet and, for once, luck was on my side. I was locked up in solitary for the final weeks of my sentence, but I didn't get any extra time added to my tariff.

Later, Frankie battered a young con who had the temerity to criticise him for his protests. It was in the canteen when we were queuing for our slops. The youngster, some meathead transferred from up north for troublemaking, made some comments to his mates thinking he was out of earshot. Frankie had a very sharp sense of hearing and immediately turned and asked the young geezer who the hell he thought he was. 'Fuck off, granddad,' was his only response.

Carefully, thoughtfully even, Frankie took off his glasses and handed them to another prisoner. Then, before the bloke could say another word, he picked up his canteen tray and swung it into the lad's throat with an almighty crack. The hard plastic edge hit him in the windpipe, and he crashed to the floor gasping like a landed fish. Frankie put his spectacles back on and calmly continued queuing for his lunch. It was a masterclass in prison etiquette from one of the true legends of the system.

I kept my head down from then on, and, on the day of my

release, Stevie Sawyer picked me up outside the heavy Wandsworth gates in a Rolls-Royce along with Arnie Fouste and Billy Gibney. I was delighted to be out but Arnie broke some unwelcome news. My former bird Maureen had been dumped by her copper and was back in London. She was working nights at the Lesney toy factory in Hackney and living with her mum in Stratford. I cursed my bad luck and hoped I could avoid her but it was blindingly obvious our paths would cross sooner or later.

It was a few months later that we finally bumped into each other at a bus stop. I'm not proud of my actions but I saw red and spat in her face.

She started crying and begged: 'Micky, please don't hurt me.'

Doing so had never entered my mind. I'd never hit a woman and wasn't about to start now.

'Maureen,' I told her, 'you're simply not worth it.'

'Please, Micky,' she pleaded, 'give me another chance. I love you, I honestly do.'

I was seeing Janet Eaton now, who I eventually married, but Maureen was gorgeous and I still loved her even though she had betrayed me for a cop. We ended up going to a motel in Forest Gate. After a few drinks, we went to our room and made love most of the night. In the morning, she begged to see me again so I agreed.

'Same time, same place next week.'

Despite our chemistry, it was hard being with her. I couldn't help thinking about the copper she had betrayed me with. What did he look like? What was his name? It was eating me alive and, after about six weeks, I knew I had to end our affair and make things work with Janet. I'd never be happy with Maureen.

On our last date I broke the news. I was brutally honest. Maybe I was too honest. 'Maureen, I've got to stop seeing you,' I told her, and the waterworks started.

'I want to try and make a go of it with Janet and I can't forget how you left me for a copper when I was inside.'

Through her tears, she asked to see me one last time, the following Friday, and stupidly I agreed.

On the Wednesday, I sat down and wrote her a letter; I'd changed my mind and just couldn't see her again. It was too difficult, I wrote, but I promised we'd stay in touch and be friends. I posted it through her mum's door the next day and forgot about it. Then I saw her again at a bus stop. She had had my letter but pleaded with me to see her one last time. She seemed better, more with it, so like an idiot I agreed, and we arranged to meet the next day at Plaistow station.

We took a cab over the river to the Ferndale pub in Woolwich, owned by an old pal of mine named George Reed. The boozer was packed and everyone was surprised to see me drinking with Maureen. My friends all knew she'd dumped me for a policeman while I was doing time – an unforgivable offence in their eyes if not mine. There was a singer in the pub – it was a proper East End knees-up – and, at the end of the night, she led me down towards the river.

We made love on the end of the old Woolwich Pier for a last time. It was sensational, as ever, but while I was getting dressed I told her we couldn't see each other again. Maureen never replied, never said a single word.

With my back to her, buttoning up my shirt, all I heard was a splash and then I realised she'd gone over the side into the Thames. She couldn't swim and was being dragged under by the currents in the dark, cold water. I dived in after her. I was a powerful swimmer, but the current was too strong and I never reached her in time. She didn't cry out once. Just slipped away.

It took me 10 minutes to get back on to dry land and I almost didn't make it myself. I pulled myself out and on to my hands and knees, and I wept. I was shaking and in shock, shivering from the cold and half-drowned myself. I couldn't believe she had killed herself. Neither would the police.

* * *

Locked up for six days without food or water and questioned day and night, I was forced to drink from the toilet to survive. This time the cops were determined to nail me and were gunning for a murder charge.

They wasted no time in reading me my rights. 'Michael Glückstad, I'm arresting you on suspicion of the murder of Maureen Wright. You are not obliged to say anything but what you do say may be taken down and given in evidence.'

I'd been stripped naked and thrown into a damp cell after calling my parents and Janet to tell them what had happened and then turning myself in at Woolwich police station to report Maureen's death.

The local bobbies wasted no time in calling in Scotland Yard's murder squad, as I knew they would, and the river was dragged for Maureen's body. It finally turned up days later. By then there was no way of proving she had thrown herself into the river. Her beautiful body was almost unrecognisable, swollen and bruised where it had been hit by the near-constant river traffic. You never look at the Thames the same way after they pull out someone you know.

There were no witnesses so the police had only my word that she had killed herself. They didn't believe me. They tried every dirty trick in the book to sweat a confession out of me – sleep deprivation, constant bright lights in my cell, beatings and threats to my family. They were convinced I had thrown her into the river then held her under until she drowned, and they kept moving me between nicks to disorientate and confuse me.

I was mourning a woman I had loved and, at the same time, fighting to convince the police and her family I was innocent of her murder. At the same time, I was riddled with guilt that I might have been responsible for her actions because I'd broken up with her. It was as close as I ever came to cracking under the strain.

When the police found Maureen's diary at her mum's house, they thought they had struck gold. It contained the letter I'd written from Wandsworth and my ill-judged threat that she wouldn't live to see her twenty-second birthday. By chance, she had died a week before that birthday. Now they thought they had probable cause and were ready to break out the champagne. Then they found the letter I'd written splitting up with her and promising we would remain friends. It painted a different picture – that we had been breaking up amicably. The motel owner came forward to say we'd been meeting regularly. My friends and family told the police that I'd admitted to cheating on Janet with Maureen and therefore had no reason to want her out of the way.

By now, I'd been in custody nearly a week and the murder squad was coming under severe pressure from the Home Office to charge me with murder or release me. It has all changed now, but, under the laws of the day, the police had already violated my rights by keeping me locked up for far longer than was permissible.

Finally, they bailed me until the inquest, confident that would give them the ammunition to throw the book at me for murder. As I left the police station, one of the senior murder squad cops laughed at me. 'We'll nick you at the inquest, laddie,' he said. 'You'll not walk away from this one easily.'

The police brought in a QC to represent them in front of the coroner and carry the death by misadventure result they were looking for. A succession of police officers and experts claimed over the course of the three-day hearing that I must have done it, as Maureen's family sat weeping in the back of the coroner's court. When I gave evidence, I looked them in the eye and told the court I had loved her and wished her no harm. The jury believed me and delivered an open verdict.

I wept with relief. I was a free man again and the police dropped their investigation. As I left the court, the same murder squad detective who had threatened me before leaned over and whispered: 'You killed her and we'll get you for it, Glückstad. You'll be looking over your shoulder for the rest of your life.'

For once, I had no reply. I was exhausted, emotionally and physically.

I never went to Maureen's funeral. I wanted to but it would have been too painful for her family. They had believed the police when they said I'd killed her. Afterwards, they moved away. I hope they were able to put her death behind them eventually. Even though I tried to save her, I carry some guilt for my part in it to this day. The police never forgot the case either. From then on, when they pulled me in for questioning, it was always brought up. 'C'mon, Glückstad. You killed that girl. Confess it now and we'll forget this matter.'

CHAPTER TWELVE

'HE PULLED OUT HIS UGLY LITTLE .38. I STARTED RUNNING AT HIM BUT BEFORE I COULD RIP HIS HEAD OFF HE SHOT ME AT ALMOST POINT-BLANK RANGE. THE IMPACT KNOCKED ME BACKWARDS BUT DIDN'T FLOOR ME. I CLUTCHED AT MY STOMACH AND MY HAND CAME AWAY COVERED IN DARK-RED BLOOD. I COULDN'T BELIEVE THE LITTLE BASTARD HAD FUCKING SHOT ME...'

BLOOD FEUD

Arnie Fouste had bought a new car. It was a flash motor and he loved it. But he'd been sold a pup. The engine was shot to pieces and it broke down within days. The dealer was giving him grief and refusing to refund his cash so I agreed to try to smooth things over. Arnie said his name was Tony, and the next day I went to his yard in Stratford for a chat. I hadn't been expecting trouble but Billy Gibney came along for the ride to keep me company all the same. Since we were boys, Billy and I had remained tight pals. But, while I had stuck with booze, brawling and the occasional big job, Billy had graduated on to the more serious stuff. He had got into some heavy shit involving guns and drugs and would sometimes disappear for weeks on end. I didn't want to know as long as he was OK, but it worried me.

Car dealer Tony obviously fancied himself as a player. He was a huge black geezer with a string of gold chains wrapped around his beefy neck and a Hawaiian shirt so loud it should have come with a health warning. Arthur Daley he wasn't. Despite the bling he looked hard as nails, with a flat nose and a big, square jaw. He must've topped six foot and, with his shirtsleeves rolled up, there was no hiding the powerful muscles and broad shoulders under his hideous outfit.

He was talking to a customer when we arrived so I hung back and had a look round his yard. There were some nice motors for sure, but something didn't quite seem right. Some of the colours were slightly off and the lines didn't look clean. I had my suspicions but wasn't going to convict a man before I'd met him.

Within about 30 seconds, I realised he was dodgy as fuck and could not be treated like a decent, respectable member of society. He was a sick dog and someone needed to put him down. I couldn't believe this chancer could have taken in a bloke like Arnie, who'd have the rings off your fingers while shaking hands if you didn't watch him like a hawk.

When he'd finished with his customer, I walked over, offering my hand to him, explaining I'd come about Arnie's car and telling him who I was. He looked down at me like something he'd found on his shoe.

'I know you, you c**t,' he snarled. 'You might have a reputation but it means fuck all around here. Now fuck off.'

To say I was taken aback was an understatement. Some blokes will play nicey-nicey to start with, gradually turning up the pressure. Big Tony clearly didn't believe in wasting time in buttering anyone up with polite conversation. It was straight to the nuclear option. Well, if that was how he wanted to play it, it was fine by me. Maybe he was having a bad day. Well, it was going to get a lot worse.

I felt my temper rising and I smashed him in the mouth, driving his head back into a brick wall. The look on his face was priceless – he'd obviously never had to deal with a customer like me before. As he slumped forward, I grabbed him by his hair and pulled his head down, then punched him two or three times in the back of the head. He was out of it, groaning on his hands and knees. Five blokes ran from the back of the yard then stopped dead when they saw their boss on the floor. Clearly they'd expected to find him using my broken bones to pick his teeth.

They looked at each other for support then lurched towards me. Billy stepped round from the back of his motor with a menacing click. In his hands was a mean-looking pump-action shotgun. I had no idea the silly sod had been packing heat but I was glad of the support. Raising their hands, the five guys backed up slowly. Big Tony had pulled himself to his feet and nodded them away.

'You'll get your money back,' he muttered.

Arnie was well pleased.

Later, I heard that Tony and his firm had been cutting and shutting cars: that is, taking smashed-up motors and putting them back on the road, sometimes using the remains of two or more badly damaged cars that have been written off by the insurers to make a new whole. That was why some of the cars in his yard showed signs of having been tampered with structurally or resprayed. They looked OK to the naked eye, but they could be death traps.

Afterwards, we passed the word around that Big Tony was to be avoided at all costs and eventually he went bust.

* * *

By the time I got shot, I must've started believing my own hype, or thinking I had become unkillable. I wasn't, and I very nearly lost my head as a result. Life was good. I was 29 years old, had just fought – and beaten – Roy Shaw, and my relationship with Janet was going well for once. I'd made a fair bit of money and was driving a nice car. My family, and Janet's, thought I was a successful businessman, buying and selling, and I hadn't done anything to disabuse them. And I still had all my own hair. There was just one blip on an otherwise cloudless horizon. A little mug called Nicky Gerard, a gangster and enforcer with a nasty reputation, who'd taken against me and had been telling friends of mine he was going to kill me.

I never got to the bottom of his beef with me. His dad was Alfie Gerard, a tough former gangland boss. There had been bad blood between Nicky Gerard and me since I'd broken the jaw of one of his pals at the Norseman club in Canning Town. I'd been having a quiet drink with a girl one evening when this bloke started trying to chat her up. He was drunk so I politely asked him to leave us alone. Instead, he smashed his beer bottle and lunged at my face. I saw it coming and ducked back in time as the jagged edge flashed past my eyes.

I would've been blinded if he'd connected and I couldn't afford to give him another shot. I grabbed his arm and slammed it into the table, loosing his hold on the bottle, then pulled back my fist and belted him as hard as I could in the mouth. He went down like a sack of shit with a broken jaw. Anyone would have done the same but it caused a right old stink with Nicky Gerard. Later, I bedded his girlfriend when he was away. I wasn't afraid of him. Gerard knew he didn't stand a chance against me in a straight-up fight.

That wasn't what brought things to a head, though. Some people reckon it was over the pool tables we were both putting into pubs. You didn't need a licence to put a table or a gaming machine in a pub or café in those days and I was making a fair bit from cashing in on the pool craze from America. It was all going nicely until Gerard wanted to push in on the protection side. Get my pool tables out of pubs double quick and his own in. He'd ripped some of the cloths on my tables to send me a message. That cost me money and I wasn't pleased. Gerard was friends with Ronnie Knight and reckoned himself well connected. We had words and I probably gave him a slap but by no means had I expected things to go nuclear.

He wasn't a big bloke but Gerard fancied himself a hard man and boasted constantly when he was drunk how he was a professional assassin. The police had him in the frame for at least one killing but couldn't prove it. People didn't like him but they were scared of him. He was unpredictable and caused trouble round the neighbourhood, especially when he had been drinking. I have no idea if he had any murders to his name. In my book, anyone who starts mouthing off about having taken a life is simply a mug who is begging to get nicked and banged up for it. Boasting like that doesn't make you hard or feared – it makes you an easy target for the Old Bill and they like nothing better. I reckoned it was only a matter of time before Gerard got a tug, and I was prepared to be patient.

That was until rumours started circulating that Gerard wanted me dead and was going to shoot me. At first, I thought nothing of them – Gerard was a gobshite – but then I was having a quiet drink with friends when I took a call from Billy Gibney. The Fonz told me Gerard had come round his house earlier that evening wild-eyed and threatening to kill me. He'd bashed on Billy's door and warned him: 'You tell Glückstad I'm going to shoot him, all right? I've got a gun here and, when I see him, he's dead.'

'All right, Nicky,' replied Billy, 'I'll tell him but you're making a mistake.'

'No,' he said. 'Glückstad's made a mistake messing with me.'

Billy Gibney was not easily scared, but Gerard had pulled the gun – a .38 revolver – out of his pocket to show he was serious. A .38 could pack a powerful punch at close range if you had the front to use it and Billy thought Gerard had.

'I think he means it, Mick,' Bill told me. 'You'd better watch your back. Let me know if you want some help sorting this out.'

'Thanks, Bill,' I said, 'I'll be fine. I appreciate the warning but I'll sort this out – he's not going to shoot anyone, let alone me.'

Outwardly I was calm, but my mind was whirring. Would Gerard really shoot me? I had plenty of friends and knew that, if he did me, one of them would certainly do him – Butch Cassidy and the Sundance Kid-style. No, I wasn't worried about that, but obviously I didn't want to get shot either. I thought on balance he was probably drunk and leery and would calm down when he sobered up. I thought I'd better go and see him to try to smooth things over rather than letting them fester. Open wounds in the East End had a nasty habit of going septic – and that usually meant someone got killed. I didn't want that. Especially not if it was me with a big bullseye painted on my forehead.

I drank up and told my pals I was off home. I didn't want any of them killed on my behalf if Gerard was going to do something stupid. It was my problem and I'd sort it out myself. I didn't think the silly little sod would have the guts to pull the trigger, whatever threats he'd made. I'd faced guns before and it's not like on TV. Staring down the barrel of Jack McVitie's sawn-off had been like looking into the proverbial Black Hole of Calcutta. Once was enough for me. I didn't fancy round two but this needed to be sorted before it got out of hand.

Gerard was a creature of habit if nothing else, and that meant he'd be in the Norseman knocking back the beers and mouthing off to the regulars. I jumped in a minicab and was outside the club on the Barking Road by midnight. Paul, the doorman, was a nice old boy and knew me well.

'All right, Mick?' he asked.

'Good, thanks, Paul. Any sign of Nicky Gerard tonight?'

'Yeah, he's been here about two hours putting it away. He's at the bar with a couple of mates. Everything OK?'

'Yeah, no problem at all. Good as gold.'

'Have a good night, Mick.'

I saw the three of them before they saw me and started to cross the room to the bar. Gerard was drinking with two low-rent thugs, Bobby Stevens and Billy Knight. It was dark, smoky and crowded in the Norseman and I reckoned I could get right beside Gerard and calm things down before he saw me. Before I reached the counter, the little fucker's head jerked up like a meerkat popping out of its hole. He swung round on his stool as if following a sixth sense and spotted me coming across the room through the smoke of a hundred cigarettes.

I stopped dead and raised my hands to show I wasn't tooled up and meant no harm. It was a red rag to a bull for a man like Gerard. Before I could say a word, he pulled out his ugly little .38. I started running at him but before I could rip his head off he shot me at almost point-blank range. The impact knocked me backwards but didn't floor me. I clutched at my stomach and my hand came away covered in dark-red blood. I couldn't believe the little bastard had fucking shot me.

The adrenalin was pumping through my veins, numbing the pain even though I was losing blood fast. I stormed across the bar before Gerard could take a second shot and wrestled the gun out of his hand. It went skittering across the floor as I smacked him in the face with my elbow. Around us customers were screaming and shouting for help. It was pure pandemonium. Then there was another bang and a bullet grazed my skull. An inch lower and it would have blown my head off.

Everything was moving at the speed of light but I reckoned Stevens had fired at me. Then I felt a sharp pain in my ankle. I'd been shot a third time, definitely by Stevens, and my leg was collapsing under me as I lurched towards them. Now I was battling all three. Trying to remain upright, I lashed out left and right, fighting for my life as never before. If I wasn't quick, it was obvious I was a dead man. They would shoot me stone-cold dead.

I caught Knight right under the chin then tried to get Stevens round the throat before he could fire again. I couldn't see his gun and feared it might be digging into my gut. I needed to put him out of the game fast so I butted him across the nose, breaking it easily and showering us both with his blood. Now everything was moving in slow motion, like a movie fight scene, but I could feel a warm patch spreading across my belly from my wound. My ankle was killing me too and I feared it might give way at any second, leaving me at their mercy on the floor. I knew there wouldn't be any.

With Stevens holding his face and Knight knocked out, Gerard was bricking it. They'd put two bullets in me and I'd kept coming. Now I was going to rip his eyes out of his head and use them as fucking cocktail olives and he could see it in my face. Before I could reach him, a massive blow struck across the right side of my head, just missing my eye and nearly taking my ear off. Paul the doorman told me he'd watched horrified as Knight had tried to take my head off with a meat cleaver. Fuck only knows why he didn't try to stop him but there you are. Luckily for me, it glanced across my face, ripping the skin rather than causing serious damage to my skull.

Turning back to him, I grabbed the machete and pulled it towards me, throwing him off balance and barging him back against the bar with my left shoulder, driving him into the woodwork. It was chaos. As I bent down to retrieve the cleaver myself, Gerard grabbed his gun and smashed me across the back of the head with the butt. I was beaten to the floor.

Struggling to my feet, I went at them again, grabbing an empty bottle as a weapon. Stevens was trying to shoot, but his gun had jammed, so he threw it at me – he missed – and made a run for the door followed by Knight and Gerard.

I collapsed on to a bar stool and passed out for a few seconds, the bar lights spinning before my eyes. When I came to, the bouncer was trying to stop the bleeding from my stomach using a filthy bar towel as a makeshift compress.

'Hang on, Micky,' Paul said, 'there's an ambulance on its way.'

The Old Bill would be following close behind, no doubt.

'Fuck that,' I said, finding new strength, 'I've got to get out of here.'

'OK, Mick, let me help you.'

Then a female voice said: 'Micky, you're losing blood fast. We've got to get you to hospital or you're going to die.'

It was an old girlfriend named Gloria who had been having a quiet drink when the shooting kicked off. She helped Paul hustle me out of the door.

As I was leaving the first cop rushed in. 'Oi, where are you going?' he shouted, trying to grab me.

'Get the fuck off me,' I snarled, barging past him and out into the street.

Gloria flagged down a passing car in the Barking Road and we jumped in before the driver could blink.

'Take me to hospital, mate. I've been shot,' I gasped.

Despite his shock, the poor bloke rushed me to Queen Mary's hospital in Stratford, breaking all the speed limits to get us there. I suppose he was terrified I might die in the back of his motor. By the time I got through the hospital doors, I had lost more than six pints of blood and was very pale and starting to shake with cold.

The doctors rushed me into the operating theatre. They sewed me up with 18 stitches in the side of my head where I'd been hit with Billy Knight's cleaver and 25 in my scalp where the second bullet had narrowly avoided taking my head off. But they couldn't dig out Gerard's first bullet. It was sitting at the base of my spine and I could have been paralysed if they dug through the muscle and it didn't heal properly. I was stuck with it. On the bright side, they told me I'd have probably bled to death in the Norseman if it had come out of my back.

So they stitched me up and gave me morphine for the pain. I've still got that bullet inside me and, every single day I've looked in the mirror since then, Billy Knight's scar has stared right back at me reminding me never to take anything or anyone for granted. My ankle was badly smashed up and they did their best to set it. When I came round, the surgeon told me in his posh accent: 'I'm sorry, Mr Glückstad, but you'll never walk on that foot again.'

I thanked him for saving my life but said: 'You're wrong about that. I'll walk again.'

The doctor replied: 'Sorry, son. I know it's hard to accept but you won't.'

In five days, I was standing, despite the excruciating agony from the wounds to my stomach and ankle. My friends and family rallied around me like never before and the doctors couldn't believe the progress I made. I was still young and fit but I surprised them nonetheless with the speed of my recovery. Perhaps the attractive young nurses helped. There was little else to be jolly about but they kept me smiling.

Six weeks later, I came out of hospital on crutches to the applause of the doctors and nurses and straight into the arms of the police. I was in custody for nearly 24 hours but I never grassed on Gerard or his mates. The police tried everything short of locking me up for obstructing the course of justice but I wasn't going to squeal. They claimed I'd been trying to extort money from Gerard – that was a laugh. I told them I'd been having a quiet drink and must've leaned on a passing bullet or two by accident. They laughed at that. Fortunately for them, there were more than 70 witnesses in the Norseman that night and many of them came forward to finger Gerard and his two pals.

That didn't stop Nicky's old man, Alfie Gerard, trying to put the frighteners on me via a mutual friend.

'Tell Glückstad to leave England and not testify or we'll kill him,' he said.

The message arrived loud and clear, but my response was forthright.

'Fuck them,' I replied via the friend. 'What do these people think? That I'm a grass or something? I'm staying put.' And I did.

I didn't fear the Gerards and sat tight in Canning Town where I was living. I spent the next few months resting and improving my walking as well as watching my back. One night a petrol bomb came through my window but I was out and it caused fuck-all damage. It was a message from the Gerards. I wasn't listening.

Word went back that I wasn't going to grass and, if it came to a fight, I wasn't going to lose either. Things quietened down a bit after that, thankfully. I didn't fancy a proper feud, though I would never have backed down. To get back in shape, I'd go to blocks of new flats in Silvertown and walk up and down the stairs until I was gasping for breath to build up my stamina and the muscles in my leg and foot. It was agony. But it worked. In six months, I was walking almost as well as before. It wasn't perfect but it was good enough. I wasn't a cripple.

I'd avoided the police as long as I could but, eventually, they subpoenaed me to testify in Gerard's trial for my attempted murder. If I didn't attend court, I'd be arrested and face a fine of several thousand pounds. OK, if they wanted it that way I'd turn up, but I was keeping my real opinions to myself.

At the Old Bailey, I told Mr Justice Melford Stevenson: 'These men are my friends, your honour. They were trying to help me. I don't know who shot me. It was dark and I couldn't see a thing. I wasn't able to identify my attackers.'

The judge turned red and started spluttering about threatening me with a perjury charge. If I'd grassed, I doubt I'd be here today. In the underworld's code of honour, turning grass was the greatest betrayal. Instead, I was treated as a hostile witness by the court.

Without my testimony, Gerard was cleared of attempted murder but got seven years for grievous bodily harm. The court heard that Gerard's missus had been sent a funeral wreath – sent to warn him to stay silent – while he was inside awaiting trial. It had nothing to do with me, but it must've worked because he refused to tell the court why he had attacked me.

Sentencing Gerard, a clearly peeved Melford Stevenson told the court: 'Mystery surrounds this attack. But it was dreadful violence of the kind which at times occurs among East End criminals.'

Bobby Stevens disappeared and was never seen again.

Incredibly, Billy Knight was found not guilty and kept his head well down after that.

A couple of years later, I was on remand in Brixton prison for burgling an office and stealing a safe containing £6,000 – the cops had nailed me on the basis of a single fingerprint – when two detectives came to see me with a proper story to tell. Nicky Gerard had long been the prime suspect in the killing of underworld enforcer Alfredo Zomparelli and now they wanted to nail him for the hit.

Known as 'Eyetie Tony' among his friends, Zomparelli worked for 'Italian' Albert Dimes, considered by the FBI to be the Mafia's man in London. He was well connected but had made enemies, falling out badly with Ronnie Knight and stabbing Knight's brother David to death during a fracas in a Leicester Square nightclub. In his biography, *Living Dangerously*, Knight swore he would see Zomparelli murdered in revenge, writing, 'for with him alive, the hate in me would eventually kill me as well'.

But Knight did not have to carry out his revenge in person. One day Gerard, who by chance was seeing Zomparelli's wife, a former stripper called Rozanna, came into Knight's Soho club with a proposition. He would keep Knight clean by doing the job for him. On 4 September 1974, Zomparelli was shot dead in the Golden Goose on Old Compton Street. A couple of days later, the cops continued, they knew Gerard had received a thick envelope from Knight. Gerard and Knight had been arrested and charged but both had been acquitted.

Now sitting in an interview cell in Brixton, the cops came to the point. They wanted the bullet out of my back. They were full of bounce and thought they could get a conviction against Gerard if they could forensically match the bullet from my back with those that killed Eyetie Tony. In return, the Flying Squad would lose the files on whatever I was accused of this time. They thought it was a good deal. I nearly fell off my chair in shock. It wasn't going to happen and I soon put them straight.

I told them in no uncertain terms: 'Apart from anything else, removing that bullet could leave me paralysed.'

'Listen to us, Glückstad,' they whispered, 'you hate Gerard. He'll never see the light of day if we can get him for the Zomparelli murder.'

'No, you listen to me,' I replied. 'Gerard's a scumbag but I'm not a grass. I didn't grass when I got shot and I'm not going to grass now. And I'm not going to risk being crippled by your half-arsed plan either. Sorry, but that's the way it is.'

Not so full of themselves now, they left and I got two and a half years when my case came to court. *C'est la vie.*

But that wasn't the end of my dealings with Gerard.

He had been out of the nick for five months in June 1982 when someone blew his head off with a shotgun outside the Spread Eagle pub in Stratford. He'd been at a birthday party for his little girl, who was 11, and was getting into his car outside the pub when he was beaten and shot. His balaclava-clad killers chased him down the street before breaking the butt of a shotgun on his skull 50 yards from his front door and finishing him off execution-style with three final blasts to the head and body. The two men left no evidence bar a Ford Cortina parked three roads away.

Some people, including the Old Bill, thought I'd pointed the gun. By chance, I left the country the next day for a trip to Denmark with some mates. When I phoned home, my wife told me the police had a warrant out for me and the *News of the World* was reporting that I was the number-one suspect. I was in Copenhagen for six days on the corner game and came home with plenty of money but no desire to be banged up. Janet picked me up off the bus at Whipps Cross and took me straight down the police station. I was locked up for two days before the cops admitted there wasn't a scrap of evidence against me and had to let me go.

Later, it was revealed that Gerard had known he was being watched, but thought it was undercover police keeping tabs on him. The *Daily Express* reported in June 1982: 'He had been out of jail only five months and felt in no danger from the men, whom he took to be officers of Scotland Yard's Criminal Intelligence Bureau.'

No one ever got nicked for the Gerard killing and I doubt anyone mourned him either. He was a nasty little toerag who honestly got what he deserved. I was disappointed because I'd have liked to have done him myself the old-fashioned way, on the cobbles with my fists, but that's the way life goes sometimes.

After me, the cops also tried to finger Tommy Hole – another well-known East End face who'd served time for armed robbery, car theft, forgery, drug manufacturing and dealing – for Gerard's murder but couldn't make that stick either when an identity parade failed to identify him as one of the shooters. Seventeen years later, Hole and his crony Joey 'The Crow' Evans were shot dead as they watched football at the Beckton Arms in Canning Town one Sunday afternoon. Two men walked up behind Evans, who was sitting at the bar with Hole, and shot him twice in the back of the skull at point-blank range, killing him instantly in front of horrified drinkers. Hole's survival instincts kicked in and took him off his bar stool and towards the pub's back door at a fair clip. He wasn't fast enough. The two killers fired at least nine shots, hitting Hole four times in the upper body and once in the head, and he collapsed in a pool of blood. Cool as you like, they turned and left the pub, disappearing discreetly through the nearby A13 underpass and into the labyrinth of dark streets beyond.

Even though the shooting happened on a busy Sunday afternoon, the police were surprised at the lack of witnesses. Some things never change in East London, I suppose. Rumours were that the two men were killed in revenge for Gerard's death all those years earlier. The local newspaper claimed Hole had recently been seen at the funeral of Gerard's uncle, James, bragging to mourners about how he had yet to be taken to account for the murder of Nicky.

I have no idea if that's true. Enough of Hole's friends said it was a pack of lies for the paper to retract its story. But, if so, it shows how East End blood feuds can last a lifetime and never end happily for anyone.

CHAPTER THIRTEEN

'THE GANGSTERS I KNEW RAN THEIR WIVES RAGGED. THE BOOZE, THE BIRDS AND THE BIRD – PRISON TIME – JUST AREN'T CONDUCIVE TO A HAPPY MARRIAGE. ADD IN THE OLD BILL BASHING DOWN THE DOOR AT ALL HOURS OF THE DAY AND NIGHT AND THE FINANCIAL UNCERTAINTY AND YOU'VE GOT A TINDERBOX SITUATION...'

TYING THE KNOT TIGHT

Less than two months after my near-fatal shooting, I was getting married. I'd met Janet Eaton a few years earlier when Billy Gibney was going out with a Turkish girl from Islington and we double-dated. Janet was her friend. She was feisty and gorgeous, my type right down to her blonde hair and sexy blue eyes, and we hit it off immediately. Billy split with the Turkish girl soon after but Janet and I started dating seriously. We were both 23 at the time and she had recently moved to London from Manchester. I loved her northern accent. In fact, I loved everything about her at the start – enough to stop me from so much as looking at another woman for a while. After that, we were on and off, but we'd always come back to each other.

I was doing very well at the time and had the appearance of a smart young East End businessman, even though I was making my money from crime and the corner game. Janet and I were to stay together for a decade before my cheating, drinking and regular run-ins with the police finally drove her away for good. When she unexpectedly got pregnant, I sorted her out with a flat, but, looking back over the years, I just wasn't ready to settle down and call it a day on my bachelorhood.

Instead of drawing us closer, the pregnancy sent me looking for escape in the arms of other women and Janet was left at home while I spent my days and nights boozing with my pals, doing my own thing and not giving a fuck about the consequences. Even so, I would love to have been there at the hospital when our son was born, four years after we first met. Janet named him Michael, after me. As it was, I didn't get the chance. I was inside for robbery and didn't meet him until he was a bouncy toddler who had no idea who this strange man called Dad was. Sadly, I carried on treating his mum abysmally.

I didn't rub it in her face but I was serially unfaithful. I was living life to the full and fancied myself as an East End playboy. Janet initially never knew what I did for a living but she didn't like violence and must have guessed. Janet had been up north visiting her mother when I was shot and raced back to be at my hospital bedside. She was there every step of the way through my recovery, helped me learn to walk again, and was by my side when I finally limped out of hospital months later. I never told her why I was shot, just said it was a case of wrong place, wrong time. And she never asked after that. Or about anything. As long as there was food on the table and money in her purse she was happy.

For a while, so was I, and when she started talking about us getting married 'for the sake of Michael', I wondered how bad it could be.

Three weeks after I came out, we were married at Stratford registry office. We were both 30 and Billy Neal, my brother-in-law, was my best man. I owned a claret-coloured Rolls-Royce Corniche that had cost me four grand and we posed for pictures in front of it with our friends and family.

Janet looked gorgeous. I was wearing a sharp brown suit and the scar caused by Billy Knight's cleaver is clearly visible – a long red line across my right cheek from under my nose to my ear. But otherwise I look like any other prosperous businessman on the make. My hair was cut short and I was wearing a white carnation in my buttonhole. With our flared trousers and wide lapels, we were a typical young couple in the late seventies. Despite all this, looking back at the pictures today, I can sense the tension between us, something I couldn't quite put my finger on at the time.

For a while, I had a very nice life, though. I had a comfy flat, a wife and son, and I owned a Roller. I was doing all right for myself living by my wits and I treated Mum and Dad, who were still going strong, whenever I could. They never asked what I'd done to get the money. If they suspected, they never said a word. If I gave Mum and Dad £1,000, I'd tell them I had a win on the horses.

My brother and sisters knew a bit about what I was up to. I conned some of John's mates who ran pubs. I made seven grand one time selling dodgy booze that didn't exist. My brother came to me and asked me if I'd taken them for a ride.

I told him: 'If they want to give me seven grand that's their lookout. It's finished. End of story.'

He didn't like it but there was no comeback on John, thankfully. He became a mechanic and never strayed. He looks like me, only a smaller version, but we've never been mistaken – luckily for him. I was the only crook in my family. The rest of them were straight as arrows, hardworking and even paid their taxes on time.

I'd been in and out of nick and by my early thirties had stolen and spent more money than most people will earn in a lifetime. My family have always supported me, every one of them. Mum and Dad used to roll their eyes at me when I was in trouble for fighting as a kid, but they knew I wasn't a bully.

They never judged me and never raised a hand to hit me. I was a very happy-go-lucky kid who never looked for trouble. But, if someone started on me, I'd never walk away. When I was sent to Kidlington for smacking the teacher, it was because he had done my brother, and I'd given him a clump in return. They understood that.

I'm glad my family are straight, if I'm honest. One of us Glückstads on the wrong side of the law is probably enough.

While my family was strong, life with Janet wasn't always going so well.

There is a myth that underworld marriages are some of the strongest around. That's a load of rubbish. Lenny McLean's wife Val might have stuck by him through good and bad and even wrote a book about their relationship called *Married to the Guv'nor*, but she was the exception that proved the rule.

Most of the gangsters I knew ran their wives ragged. The booze, the birds and the bird – prison time – just aren't conducive to a happy marriage. Add in the Old Bill bashing down the door at all hours of the day and night and the financial uncertainty and you've got a tinderbox situation. Some women might adapt. Most never will.

Janet and I rattled on for another three years but in the end my behaviour drove her away. I'm not proud of it but, in retrospect, marriage was a mistake. It didn't bring us closer together; it highlighted the fault lines in our relationship. We didn't talk enough and I wasn't there for my family when the crunch came. I was a bit of a playboy, out painting the town red at all hours of the day and night, fighting and, more than I liked, doing time inside prison.

Our son Michael will be in his late thirties now and we haven't spoken for years. He stuck with Janet when we finally split up and they moved away. It's one of the few things I regret. But that's life, I suppose.

Maybe if he reads this he'll get in touch, and we'll go for a drink and have a chat like father and son, but somehow I doubt it.

While my relationship with Janet was going well, I didn't see as much of my pals. When we were arguing, I was out and about with the lads. The old gang of East End schoolmates stuck together through thick and thin.

Outside Danny Woollard's Manor Park club, the Hathaway,

was a phone box. There was nothing wrong with that on the face of it – in fact, it was quite handy in the days before mobile phones for calling a cab or doing some business.

What was causing a problem was a fat black woman who appeared from the neighbouring estate at 3am nearly every day and spent at least 30 minutes shouting obscenities, screaming and crying down the phone line. It soon became clear that she never put money into the phone. She was talking to herself.

At first, Danny laughed about it. But the longer it went on, the more problems it caused. The woman's yelling was keeping the neighbours awake and causing problems for Danny's licence, even though it had nothing to do with him. When anyone complained, the woman would abuse them and her three large sons, who fancied themselves as wannabe villains, would visit the next day and threaten them with a beating.

After a couple of months, Danny could take no more and we decided to have a bit of fun with the woman. One night at about 2.50am, I sneaked out to the phone box and covered the receiver with superglue, really lathered it on. Ten minutes later, like clockwork, up waddles the woman, picks up the phone and begins shouting her usual obscenities.

After a couple of minutes, she realised something was wrong. Danny and I were watching from the window of his club. Her ear and hand were stuck fast to the receiver and she panicked.

She screamed, cried and shouted until finally someone called the police. The coppers were cracking up laughing. No one could do anything until an ambulance and then a fire engine came and the phone cord was cut away. The last we saw of her she was being led to the ambulance. Danny and I were in hysterics.

The next day, the joke turned a bit sour. The woman's three sons were rampaging around the estate trying to find out who glued their mum to the phone, smacking people up and generally making a nuisance of themselves. They finally frightened someone into telling them Danny and I were responsible for ambushing their mad mother with the superglue.

That afternoon I was playing pool with Danny inside the Hathaway when the brothers walked in. Fortunately, a pal of Danny's had tipped him off that they were tooled up and looking for us so we were ready for them.

Danny had asked me: 'Can't they take a fucking joke?' The answer, apparently, was no.

They'd told Danny's mate they were going to bury us. They weren't messing about. They strolled into Danny's club like they owned the place and went straight over to the pool table. I'd never seen them before and they were big, nasty-looking bastards. The biggest of the three asked: 'Are you two the arseholes who fucked with our mum?'

Neither of us said anything. I could see the bloke's hand twitching in his pocket. He had either a gun or a knife. I wasn't taking any chances. I leaned down to take my shot, then, without warning, whipped the pool cue up and smashed the bloke over the bridge of his nose with a crunch. The cue smashed in half and blood spurted out of his face. He dropped a knife he'd been reaching for as he brought his hands to his face to cup his shattered nose. Before he could move, I whacked him twice around the back of the head to take him out of the game.

The other two stood gobsmacked as their brother fell screaming to his knees. Now they started to react. It was too late. Danny had two pool balls in a sock and as brother number two started towards me he smashed him as hard as he could. The missile caught the thug in the mouth with a thud and he fell like he'd been poleaxed, blood and broken teeth spilling everywhere from his ruined mouth.

The third brother thought fast and made a run for it. I chased him out of the club. He had a bit of fight in him but I decked him and kicked him hard to make sure he wasn't going to get up any time soon. As I was finishing him off, Danny dragged the other two muppets out of the club and locked up. Then we called the cops. In the end, the brothers were carted off by ambulance and another fire engine was called to hose the blood from the pavement.

We thought the brothers wouldn't grass as they fancied themselves as up-and-coming villains. The next morning at 6am the cops kicked down my door. Danny got raided at the same time. They were confident we were going away. We denied everything and were given three weeks' police bail. In the event, the brothers couldn't pick us out of an identity parade. They told the police the men they thought had been Micky Glückstad and Danny Woollard were nothing like us. We weren't charged and the brothers kept a low profile after that. It seems they had decided they weren't that bothered about being villains after all.

That was the problem in the East End at the time. There was always someone trying it on. One of the worst was Micky Jamieson. His dad, 'Scotch' Eddie, was a decent man with a terrible temper. He never started a fight in his life but, when upset, he was merciless. He had 11 sons who wanted to be like him – none of them matched up to their old man to my mind. But the worst was Micky Jamieson. He had no class and no bottle. He was a bully. One night I was due to meet Danny Woollard in the Duke of Edinburgh pub in Green Street, Upton Park. I was early and having a quiet drink on my own at the bar when who should roll in but Micky Jamieson.

The bloke just couldn't keep his mouth shut. The minute he saw me he barrelled over and started giving it the big gob. 'Who do you think you are, Glückstad? You're a mug, you are. I'm gonna take your head off, mate.'

'Leave it, Micky,' I said, 'you're drunk and looking for a fight but I'm not interested.'

A normal bloke would have got the message. As I turned back to my pint, I caught a flash of steel in the corner of my eye. Jamieson had pulled a knife and lunged at me. If I'd been a millisecond slower he'd have skewered me in the back. Luckily, he was half-cut and slow. I grabbed his wrist and wrenched the knife away with my left hand, then smacked him straight on the chin with my right. It was a good shot and he went down unconscious between the bar stools.

His mate should've known better but didn't. He picked up his pint and dived at me, smashing it over my head. You're a brave man if you raise a weapon to me – or very stupid. With blood pouring down my face, I grabbed him by the scruff of the neck and smacked him hard a couple of times until he was out cold too.

Five minutes later, when Danny arrived, I'd finished my pint and had a bar towel wedged against my head to try to stop the bleeding.

I joked: 'Welcome, Mr Woollard. Just in time to take me to hospital!'

The look on his face was priceless. Me at the bar, the two slags on the floor – broken glass, blood and beer everywhere. I had 15 stitches and was back in the pub before closing time with Danny.

When we arrived, Scotch Eddie was holding court in the bar and not happy. He didn't waste any time with small talk. 'My boy's in hospital with a broken jaw. I've been told three of yous done him. Is that right?' he asked.

'Eddie, he tried to stab me first,' I told him. 'Then his mate done me with a glass. Ask anyone in here. They'll put you straight.'

Eddie was old school and understood so we had a drink instead of a fight.

His boy came to a nasty end, but not before he'd screwed up a lot of other lives. A few months after our run-in, an old couple in Canning Town won £1,000 on the bingo. Jamieson and a pal followed them home, broke in and tortured them to death for the money. When the police cornered him he cried like a coward.

He got life with a recommendation he serve at least 30 years for murder and other offences including armed burglary, but he couldn't handle life inside and killed himself in his cell at Full Sutton prison in York at the age of 33. His family were decent people and didn't deserve that, but he was a bad apple all right.

CHAPTER FOURTEEN

'HE CAME AT ME QUICKLY FOR SUCH A LARGE MAN. BUT I WAS QUICK TOO, AND CRASHED MY FIST INTO HIS CHIN FOLLOWED BY A BLOW TO HIS RIBS. YOU COULD SEE HIS SURPRISE. SMALLER BLOKES LIKE ME WEREN'T SUPPOSED TO FIGHT BACK. THEY WERE SUPPOSED TO TAKE THEIR BEATING, TIP THEIR HAT AND CRAWL AWAY BLEEDING...'

TEACHING THE GUV'NOR A LESSON

Lenny McLean was a liberty taker and a bully. I don't like to talk ill of the dead – and I don't want to upset his family – but there it is. I'm not going to lie just because he's some kind of big name. He might have been the Guv'nor and he might have been a very hard man but he picked on the old and weak. In my book, that's plain wrong and I don't take that from anyone. The Lenny McLean legend might make good reading but it's not the man I knew and fought twice on the cobbles. He was an actor and a good one. He had a lot of front and made the best of what he had been given. That gave him a pretty good living scaring people witless.

I can't condemn a man for wanting to put bread on the table but I can't abide bullies either and he was an old-school steal-your-dinner-money bully. When he was working as a doorman, McLean would pick on some old boy sozzled with drink, or a youngster out with his mates and barely old enough to shave, let alone stand toe to toe with a hard man. He wouldn't pick on someone his own size. Because of that, I had little respect for him. There were many hard men who knew the difference between right and wrong and treated people respectfully. McLean wasn't one of them. He was a year younger than me but we were both working-class lads who grew up a couple of miles apart in straitened circumstances during the austerity period, him in Hoxton, and me in Plaistow, but that's where all similarity ends.

He was battered black and blue by his stepfather – a truly horrible c**t by all accounts – and it made him mean. I had a loving family who never judged me once and certainly never raised a hand to me. Whatever else I did, I never threw my weight around. I'm going to sound like a fucking sociologist now but it shows that if you grow up in a broken home and facing violence it can turn you nasty.

The way people talk about Lenny McLean in hushed tones, you'd think he was some sort of East End folk hero, but he was never popular. People were scared of him, for sure, but they didn't like him. He was a second-rate thug who had a first-rate publicity machine when he became famous. Half of his book was nonsense. He said he had 3,000 fights and never lost one. You'd be fighting every day of your life if that were the case. But the legend 'I look what I am, a hard bastard' was absolutely true. He was a very hard man indeed.

The problem was he used his strength and size to intimidate others. He doesn't write about that in his book. I had never heard of him when we first met.

Undoubtedly there will always be those who will abuse me for slagging off McLean. He's not here to answer his critics, you're cashing in on his fame, and you never beat him. The type of behind-your-back, never-to-your-face criticism that weak, sneaky people love. Well, firstly, I couldn't give a fuck. And, secondly, I was there. I fought the man and beat him – twice. Ironically, I cost myself a fair old pot of money by battering the muppet outside the ring.

When he was a big name, you could challenge him for a purse of £10,000 minimum. I never took a penny for bettering him with my fists. Not that I'm complaining. I never walked away from a fight and never will. And I'm not going to lie. It gives me pleasure recalling how I thumped him when he tried to put the frighteners on a good friend of mine who was minding his own business.

My pal Stevie Sawyer was running the Green Man in Hoxton market when he asked me to come over and sort out a problem. Some geezer had been in, throwing his weight around and trying to take protection money off him. As usual with a mate, I didn't ask questions; I dropped everything and went to find out what was what. I didn't know the geezer's name then, but it was Lenny McLean.

'This huge bloke's been coming in,' Stevie told me, 'pushing me about and demanding a share of the takings in return for running the door.'

The Green Man was a proper old-fashioned boozer in the old market area of Hoxton and attracted a rough crowd at times. Stevie wasn't a shrinking violet and he didn't need door staff. But this was an old-school protection racket.

I'd just come out of prison after doing a year for robbery and, although I didn't fancy another spell at Her Majesty's pleasure right away, was in no mood to mess about. Taking a corner table, I sat quietly with a couple of mates and we had a beer or two.

Sure enough, soon afterwards in strolls this big bloke with two mates like he's the cock of the walk and owns the place.

Leaving the barmaid to serve him, Stevie came over and said: 'There's the bloke causing the trouble – calls himself Lenny McLean and fancies himself as a right hard nut. He's making my life a misery. What do you think?'

'No problem, Stevie,' I replied. 'I'll sort this out one way or another.'

I had seen McLean clocking me as I talked to Stevie. He didn't give me a chance to talk as I walked across the bar towards him. He looked me up and down and said: 'I don't know who you are, but you've made a big mistake getting involved.'

'No, you c**t, you've made the mistake,' I replied. 'This pub's run by my mate and he doesn't need your protection so get the fuck out of here.'

Getting up, McLean told me to 'fuck myself' and pushed me. That was it. My jacket was off my back and over a chair and I fronted him up face to face.

The Guv'nor wasn't always as big as when he became famous. He was about 15 and a half stone and muscular when I first fought him. When he started training properly, he got stuck into steroids and he blew up big.

For now, he was plenty big enough though, with hands like bunches of bananas covered in steel, and he came at me quickly for such a large man. But I was quick too, and crashed my fist into his chin followed by a blow to his ribs. You could see his surprise. Smaller blokes like me weren't supposed to fight back. They were supposed to take their beating, tip their hat and crawl away bleeding.

He didn't falter, managing to pull back at the last moment and taking some of the power out of my blow as it glanced off his face. He feinted with a right hook, and then smashed his left fist into my head. I saw stars and staggered backwards, buying some time and dodging out of reach. Now he was getting cocky, lunging at me and trying to pound my ribs with a string of sharp hooks to the body.

'C'mon, you little c**t,' he screamed, spit flying.

He looked insane and it was no surprise he evoked such fear in people. His fists were flying towards me and I was seriously busy trying to dodge them before they connected and did some real damage to my internal organs. Luckily, unlike someone like Roy Shaw who'd boxed professionally, McLean's technique was all over the place. He was used to hammering hard – left, right, left – pounding his victims into submission like a pig's carcass hung from a butcher's hook.

Despite this, I wasn't fazed. I was going to give it back with interest. I parried his left with my elbow and knocked his right away with my own fist, sending him momentarily off balance. All around me it was kicking off as my pals took on McLean's and I could hear yelling and smashing glass.

Glancing over McLean's shoulder to distract him, I feinted with my left shoulder then smashed my right fist into his face. Now he had no time to pull back or sidestep and the blow caught him squarely in that broad, many-times-broken nose with a crack like thunder. It crunched under my fist and he yelled in pain and surprise. But I was already hammering him in the ribs, taking advantage of my smaller size and speed to strike some blows before he recovered his balance.

We were both puffing away like steam trains and sweat was pouring down my back. McLean was a very hard man and soaking up my punishment. I could see him gasping to himself, 'C**t, c**t, c**t,' psyching himself up as he charged forwards, arms swinging. For now, I was managing to avoid those massive fists. But one clever blow and he'd take my head off.

Lunging forward again, he wrapped his arms round my sides, trapping my arms and trying to squeeze the life out of me.

Thinking fast, I smashed my head upwards under his chin and heard him scream in anger as his jaw snapped shut and he bit his tongue. At the same time I kicked down hard on his shin with the heel of my boot.

He reeled back, releasing my arms. I took a quick look around the bar, checking that no one was about to plant me one from behind, then slammed my right fist into McLean's head, followed by my left, then another right for good measure. He was wavering so I charged him, driving him back over a table and on to the floor, where I punched and punched at his body until he raised his arms in submission. I gave him a couple of smacks for luck. My knuckles were raw and bleeding. Many men who've taken a fair kicking will react with good grace. Not McLean. Pulling himself to his feet, he swore and spat blood on the floor before being helped out of the pub by his battered and bleeding group of mates.

That was the first time I did Lenny McLean. I won't lie; it was one of the toughest fights I had. But he didn't scare me. That puffing and panting, the roaring like he was Mr Wolf trying to blow down the houses of the Three Little Pigs – it might've worked with lesser men, but not with me.

Funnily enough, he never mentioned the hiding I gave him in the Green Man in his bestselling book *The Guv'nor*. He never showed his face around there again either, let alone tried to demand protection.

But by the time I next came to blows with McLean, he was a proper crowd puller. I'll give him that. Everyone wanted to see him fight but he handpicked his opponents to make sure he didn't take on more than he could handle. At that time he was advertising for all-comers and there was a decent purse on offer for the fight, at least £10,000. I needed the money and thought, Why not? I've beaten this muppet once, I can do him again and this time get paid for the pleasure.

Even I was shocked at how much bigger McLean had got when I finally caught up with him in the bar of the White Swan in Limehouse. It's a gay pub now but back in the day the Swan was a proper spit-and-sawdust joint and saw its fair share of spilled blood and ruffled feathers.

A few words got said, and the next thing I knew we were having another fight. I can't remember who threw the first punch but I know who threw the last. I bested him again. McLean says in his book that he never lost a fight, but he's lost against a few people in and out of the ring. Just shows you can't believe everything you read.

Meanwhile, my reputation had made me a target. I enjoyed it at first, being known in the East End as a man to be feared and respected, the bloke who'd beaten Roy Shaw and Lenny McLean. Now, whenever I went out, some mug was waiting to impress his mates by giving me a hiding. The violence, threats and constant tension were killing my marriage to Janet. We loved each other but she couldn't stomach my way of life. For me, the fear of the early-morning knock at the door was like the radio in a greasy spoon – after a while you just tuned it out. Janet couldn't and the uncertainty was making her ill and miserable. The happy-go-lucky young woman I'd met years before had become a shadow, and it was my fault. It couldn't go on. Sorrowfully, we decided to call it a day and go our separate ways.

After my split with Janet, I'd started drinking more than was good for me and let myself go a bit. I was still depressed about Maureen and felt guilty about her death as well as about the end of my short-lived marriage and losing contact with my son. Friends rallied round but I didn't feel like working. All I wanted to do was lose myself at the bottom of a beer glass, but I couldn't get any peace.

Since Maureen's death, I had become a target for the police and they were harassing me constantly. Pulling over my car on any pretext, stopping me in the street, coming to my home. On top of this, I couldn't walk down the street without every Tom, Dick or Harry wannabe wide boy looking to forge their own reputation by taking me down. It was becoming harder and harder to walk away from the constant baiting. So in the end I did what I had always done – I fought back.

One night at a party in Canning Town, a big bloke started on me, winding me up and trying to get a rise out of me. He'd heard about my standing and wanted to take it away from me. He fancied his chances, too.

'You don't look that hard to me,' he said. 'I reckon I could do you.'

'You probably could, mate,' I replied. 'But you won't get the chance tonight. I'm going home.'

I turned to leave but before I could move this bloke jumped up and grabbed me in a bear hug, trying to crack my ribs. At first I played along, letting him have his fun. People were laughing and it looked like he was just messing about. But his arms were crushing me as he gripped tighter and tighter and I could feel my ribs creaking. Fuck this. I lost the plot. Leaning forward, I clamped my teeth around his nose and bit down as hard as I could.

He was screaming fit to wake the dead and dropped me but I clung on with my teeth. Blood was pouring down his face and he was sobbing. I wrenched my teeth away from his nose, taking a hunk off the tip, and spat it into an empty beer glass. The big bloke wasn't laughing now – he was on his knees sobbing, holding the torn flesh in his hands and trying to stop the bleeding.

The party had stopped dead. I looked round and asked: 'Anyone else think they can beat me?'

There was stunned silence as I picked up my blood-stained jacket from the floor where it had fallen during the fracas and walked out. The police were called and I was picked up on the way home but no one would give evidence against me, including the big bloke whose nose had been stitched together by surgeons, so reluctantly they had to release me. I have no doubt that only made them more determined to stick me inside.

Another night I was meeting some pals at a pub in Bow, East London, when a group of lads set about me without warning. The first smashed his glass into my face as the others queued up to put the boot in. I couldn't give an inch or I knew they would tear me apart so, as the bar cleared of punters, I went crazy, punching, kicking and headbutting them. I took them all on instinct alone; my survival gene kicked in and I left them battered and bleeding on the floor. Never before had I released so much aggression. They were drunk and clumsy and I was merciless. It was carnage, the bar was destroyed, windows broken and bottles smashed, and I walked away with my head held high. The next day the pub was boarded up, closed for business. Again, I was arrested but the prosecution witness didn't turn up in court so I walked free. The police thought I was laughing at them. At the time I felt I was the butt of the joke and it wasn't doing me any favours.

Shortly afterwards, I was drinking myself into a stupor in Canning Town when I was set upon by five hard men. I was all over the shop, staggering left and right and lashing out wildly, but I still managed to knock two of them down. As I hit the second bloke, I felt someone jump on my back. I swung round trying to throw him off before sheer weight of numbers told and they beat me to the floor. I thought they were going to kill me. They kicked and punched me, beat me with coshes and slashed me with razor blades. I was in a sorry state and ended up in hospital stitched together once more by the surgeons. Ironically, my boozed-up state saved me from worse injuries because the alcohol had relaxed my muscles. As usual, the police didn't want to know and I wouldn't tell them anything anyway. I'd sort this out myself.

Friends had begun making enquiries when they'd heard about my injuries and all the evidence pointed to a bloke known as Harry Boy, a right flash c**t trying to make a name for himself in the East End. We'd never come across each other so I could only guess that my reputation had, once more, got me into trouble. This time, however, it would not be sorted out over a friendly pint in a pub. There was only one way to respond to such mindless provocation, by visiting extreme retribution on my assailants and sending the message out once and for all that I was not to be fucked with by anyone. Harry and his mates drank in a wine bar in Canning Town. Billy Gibney came along as back-up. We waited outside in cars for them to get trashed so they were well drunk when we pounced. As when they had jumped me, five against one, no mercy was shown. If they wanted to be players, they would have to learn how to take a proper hiding like men.

I carried a bottle of squirt, as ammonia was known on the street, and made short work of two of them immediately, spraying it into their eyes. As they screamed in pain, momentarily blinded and helpless, it was now three against two. Billy, who would put his hand into a fire for me if I asked, was wielding a baseball bat like a man possessed, swinging wildly as if for an imaginary ball and making mincemeat out of Harry Boy's mates. The adrenalin was coursing through my veins and I concentrated on the main man, smashing him across the head with a cosh then stamping on his knee to bring him down. As he writhed on the floor, I pounded his body and face. He was a mess. I might have killed him had Billy not dragged me away, but the message was sent and received loud and clear. Now, any two-bit hood would think twice about using me to make his name.

CHAPTER FIFTEEN

'DANNY'S FACE WAS A MASS OF BRUISES, HIS HEAD LOOKED TWICE AS BIG AS NORMAL AND HE COULD BARELY SPEAK BECAUSE HIS MOUTH WAS BADLY CUT. ROY'S JAW WAS SWOLLEN AND HE HAD A BROKEN ARM, AND DANNY WOOLLARD'S NOSE WAS BROKEN BADLY AND TWICE AS BROAD AS IT SHOULD HAVE BEEN. I HAD TWO BLACK EYES AND FAIRSY WAS ON CRUTCHES AND COULD BARELY WALK, HAVING BEEN BATTERED BY THE KANGAROO. IT WAS FAIR TO SAY WE WERE A SHAMBLES...'

BOXING MATILDA

Sometimes the truth really is stranger than fiction. Like the time I got battered over a fight with a boxing kangaroo. You'll have to bear with me on this one, but it really happened. Life was that strange at times. To cut a long story short, I was drinking with pals including Danny O'Leary, Danny Woollard and Roy Hunt in the Mitre pub in Greenwich, when we met some girls. They lived in Blackheath so, hoping to impress, we offered them a lift in a big American Buick owned by another friend, Fairsy as he was known. As we were driving them home, there was a massive fairground on Blackheath itself and the girls thought it would be fun to stop.

As was common in those days, among the coconut shies and shooting galleries, there was a boxing booth where you could challenge one of the fair's prizefighters, usually a big bloke with a handlebar moustache and bulging biceps. But that was for the kids and we weren't tempted. Next door, I kid you not, was a boxing kangaroo inside a big canvas marquee. It was the centre of attention. The owner was offering £20 to anyone who could go three rounds with the animal, and doing roaring business by the looks of things. The punters were queuing up to have a pop at the bouncing beast and impress their girlfriends or mums.

Now I'd heard of boxing kangaroos, but I'd never seen one in the flesh like this.

You'd never get away with it now, for good reason – the animal rights brigade would go absolutely ballistic and you'd be up in court before you could whistle 'Waltzing Matilda'. But, in the late sixties, people had a more relaxed attitude towards animals, I suppose. From what I could see, the dusty brown kangaroo was pretty tasty in the ring. He was a whopper with a huge body and small head that was hard to connect with. He had his own gloves, and must've been at least six feet tall and about 13 stone, and he was dishing out some evil blows, using his paws and his big feet to pound his opponents.

We were pretty drunk and the girls thought the kangaroo was hilarious so I went to get into the ring with the roo. Fairsy beat me to it even though the kangaroo dwarfed him. He was only a smallish bloke, not much of a fighter, and not particularly well built either, and it took the kangaroo only a few seconds to send him flying through the ropes and straight out of the ring. The girls in particular were laughing fit to burst and I could see Fairsy's pride was badly damaged. Gamely, he climbed back in but he was being knocked all over the place.

The animal's small, hard fists were really bashing him. I noticed he was leaning back on his powerful tail then using it to spring forwards against the smaller man, driving him back and kicking and punching. It was a secret weapon and gave the animal its momentum. The roo actually seemed to be enjoying the battle. Fairsy certainly wasn't. The silly sod was regretting having climbed in.

I thought I'd better help him so, the next time the kangaroo came round the ring in front of us, Danny O'Leary and I leaned through the ropes, grabbed his tail and tried to drag him away from Fairsy. I thought we could upset his balance if we pulled it off the ground. Amazingly, it worked. The kangaroo was struggling like mad and making a wailing sound as Fairsy tried to get a few blows in and restore some badly damaged ego. The fairground folk went mad. The roo's owner was shouting and screaming at us to unhand his champion, Fairsy was yelling blue murder, and I was laughing so hard I could barely keep upright as this huge muscular tail lashed about in my arms. Next thing I knew, I'd been belted round the head from behind with some sort of cosh and Danny was being set upon by three big blokes. The fairground workers piled in and one hell of a fight kicked off. The girls went from laughing hysterically to screaming hysterically, the boxers from the booth next door piled in and suddenly it was chaos. I released the roo's tail to defend myself and, suddenly free, he sprung at Fairsy, sending him flying from the ring again.

By this time the fight had spilled outside from the big kangaroo tent. It seemed like the entire fair was involved in the mass brawl. No one knew who they were fighting but all the sideshow workers had joined in and I could see a single copper blowing furiously on his whistle to try to restore order. Some chance, mate, I thought, taking another blow to the side of my head. The girls were long gone and we were getting battered by tinkers with baseball bats and staves. Another night out had degenerated into a free-for-all. Suddenly, its horn blaring, the big black Buick came crashing through the fairground, smashing the sideshows apart and sending staff and customers diving for safety. A hoopla stall, offering goldfish if you could send a hoop over a bowl, was destroyed and the little orange fish were flapping about on the floor as the owner tried to scoop them up. A bingo stall was in pieces, with broken china, pots and pans and cuddly toys everywhere.

We all scrambled into Fairsy's car and he took off like a bat out of hell, saving us from a real hiding or worse. Those fairground folk can be properly tough, and sheer weight of numbers would have done for us badly. As it was, we had a fair few injuries. The next day we met up in a local café in a sorry state. Danny's face was a mass of bruises, his head looked twice as big as normal and he could barely speak because his mouth was badly cut. Roy's jaw was swollen and he had a broken arm, and Danny Woollard's nose was broken badly and twice as broad as it should have been. I had two black eyes and Fairsy was on crutches and could barely walk, having been battered by the kangaroo. It was fair to say we were a shambles. As Reg Kray once said: 'If you can look at yourself in the mirror when you shave each morning and like what you see, then you're OK.' Well, that morning I really didn't recognise myself.

At the time I was minding the door for my mate Mike Tucker at the Green Gate pub and nightclub in Stratford three nights a week. The money was good and the bar attracted a nice crowd generally – not too much aggro. All I had to do was keep it that way to collect 50 per cent of the door money.

One of the regulars, Billy 'The Bomb' Williams, was one of the hardest men I ever met. Billy was a Canning Town legend who, like me, was a promising young boxer who had been dogged by trouble. He was a one-punch knockout specialist with a fearsome reputation and had once sparred with Cassius Clay. He had the potential to go far, but never escaped his East End roots.

Instead, like me, he ended up in prison for armed robbery. Another time, he held a man down in the street while another fella ran over his legs in a car. I never saw that side of him but he had some rough mates; one night, after a fight, one of them stabbed a lad he was fighting through the heart outside the pub.

I saw everything from the door and called an ambulance, even though the poor bloke was dead before he hit the ground. The Old Bill arrived about the same time as the ambulance. It was too late: the victim was brown bread and going cold already. I told them I hadn't seen a thing. One of the other boys told the cops I'd been inside but I could see they weren't happy. After they carted the lad away, I sloshed down the pavement with a bucket of hot water and bleach. I'd never seen so much claret; he must've lost nearly every pint in his body as his dying heart pumped it out on to the street. I walked back inside, told Mike I was leaving and went home to a bottle of whisky.

The next day I was pulled in hung over by the murder squad as a potential witness. I told them to get fucked: I hadn't seen anything. They had their man anyway, so my refusal to point fingers never made a difference, but it didn't help my relationship with the Old Bill and I lost the door a week or so later as a result of pressure on Mike. The next night there was still a brown stain on the pavement. There were none of the flowers or teddies or candles that pop up every time some two-bit thug gets greased these days. It was better that way if you ask me. The ways things are going these days, soon every stretch of road will have its own shrine. It's crazy. The cemetery's the place for flowers and tears. Not the cobbles.

* * *

In one of the backstreets of Forest Gate was a club called the 77 in a cellar. One night, heading home, I thought I might pop in for a last drink. As I entered four black men were leaving. 'No whites, man,' one of them said. I honestly thought the bloke was joking so I stuck my head round the door. Inside, two white girls spotted me and started screaming, 'No white men allowed.' It was mad and it was racist but I didn't want trouble so I turned around and left, darting back up the stairs to the street. I wasn't fast enough. By the time I reached the pavement I was surrounded by a gang of clubbers and events were in serious danger of turning nasty.

The beer had been talking and these boys were in a dangerous mood. God only knows who'd wound them up but they were ready to tear me apart. A massive mean-looking black geezer, the club's owner, appeared to be their leader. It wasn't in me to run from a fight, no matter how heavily the odds were stacked against me. I looked him up and down – he was at least a head taller than me and probably pushing 17 stone – then, staring straight in his eye, I told him: 'I can't fight all you jokers at once. But I'll do you one at a time and win – you first, mate.'

That did it. He laughed out loud then told his pals: 'Leave this to me. Everyone stay out of it.'

Without further ado, we went toe to toe for nearly five minutes, each looking for a way of pounding seven shades of shit out of the other. At one point I thought he had me. His sheer size overwhelmed me and I'd slipped on the pavement, letting him grab me in a choke hold around the throat. He was really strong and I could feel my strength ebbing away as he squeezed tighter and tighter until I managed to free an arm and jab him in the eye. He dropped me, clutching his face and falling to one knee. This was my chance; I hammered him, punching, belting and kicking in a frenzy of violence until he was lying motionless on the ground.

Seeing their boss down and beaten badly, none of the others moved. I walked away.

A few days later, I was walking through Forest Gate when the same geezer popped up. Christ, I thought, not again, then he stuck his huge hand out.

'Put it there, Micky,' he said, 'no one's ever beaten me like that. You're welcome in my gaff any time.'

He turned out to be a decent bloke. He told me the club had suffered a series of attacks by racists, with customers beaten and paint thrown down the entrance steps. That explained my reception. After that, we were mates.

A few weeks later, I came across a good money-making opportunity, and the chance to do a pal a favour. A good friend, Tim – whose surname I won't mention here because he's a respectable and legit businessman now – was making a packet dealing cocaine to boozed-up city traders. It wasn't my scene but these boys could afford it and Tim was a decent bloke who knew when to buy a round of drinks. Anyway, unbeknown to him, the drugs squad was hot on his heels and had been keeping him under surveillance when he picked up a shipment in his new Mercedes and left it at Heathrow while he flew off to his holiday home in Spain with the missus. He figured the car and its contents would be safe in the high-security long-term car park. The cops reckoned otherwise, and towed the Merc from Heathrow back to Limehouse nick where they impounded it. At the time, the police had to search a suspect's home or vehicle in their presence. So the cops sat back, pleased as punch, and waited for a suntanned Tim to return from Spain to collar him.

We had a bit of help at Limehouse nick in those days. It wasn't cheap, a grand as I recall, but the information was good and a call came through warning us that Tim's car had been lifted and he was going to be picked up the moment he stepped off the plane at Heathrow. Tim was in a right old pickle, understandably, but we had a solution. We would spring his car from the pound and with it the cocaine. It would take some planning but it had every chance of succeeding.

I knew Limehouse police station well. The car compound was alongside the main building and surrounded by a high wire fence, but there was only a single traffic boom over the roadway. You could crawl under it easily to gain access. In honesty, for a police station the security was a joke. I don't expect they thought anyone would be stupid enough to break in. I got on the blower to Tim and sorted a spare set of keys to his car from his gaff in Barking. Then another friend sorted two stolen cars that we planned to use as mobile barricades. Finally, our good pal Barry Dalton, a former bare-knuckle fighter and minicab-firm manager, agreed to act as the getaway man. If anyone got his plate, he would tell the cops he was simply picking up a fare.

Myself, Danny Woollard, Billy Gibney and another mate of ours, Steve Savva, were going to do the job. Savva would spring the Merc, Danny and I would block the exits from the police station to stop anyone pursuing us, and Billy would be keeping watch from across the street in case anything went wrong. We had it planned to the last second and it went like a dream. Savva casually strolled into the car compound, ducked under the traffic boom, used the spare keys to get into Tim's motor then drove it out of the car pound as fast as he could, smashing through the traffic barrier like it was made of matchsticks. He was off down the road towards the Commercial Road and the backstreet lock-up we'd prepared for Tim's car.

As he whizzed off, Danny and I, wearing balaclavas and leather gloves, roared up outside the nick in our stolen cars, blocking both vehicle exits. Now the station was hemmed right in and any cops who tried to chase Savva would be stuck. We locked the wheels, jumped out and ran for it, dumping the keys down a storm drain. Our operation brought the entire nick to a complete standstill.

It was like *The Italian Job*, except without the famous Mini Coopers and not in Italy! But you get the picture.

Barry zoomed up, we leapt in and we were away.

Later that day, we met up at the lock-up. Billy retrieved the drugs for Tim and the car was resprayed, given new documents and sold off. Limehouse police went potty. Our snout told us they thought they were being attacked by the IRA when they saw Danny and me pull up in our balaclavas. The top brass were fuming and they had nothing on Tim. He was off the hook and arrived back at Heathrow the next day to find his car missing and, wait for it, called the police to report it stolen. The whole operation went like clockwork. Tim was well pleased and we were well rewarded.

Sadly, some years later, in 1992, Barry Dalton became yet another of our group of mates to meet his end prematurely. His body was found near Alexandra Palace in the same car he'd driven us away in. He'd been shot in the head at point-blank range. He had a wife and five little ones at home. Barry was a colourful character who'd once fallen out with Lenny McLean and took his revenge by turning up at his flat with a shotgun. Lenny had just got out of the shower by all accounts and opened the door wearing little more than a towel. When he saw the gun, he ran for it and Barry shot him in the arse. No one thought he meant to kill McLean, just give him a scare. To this day, Barry's murder remains unsolved.

A few months later I was arrested and charged with demanding protection money alongside Roy Neal, Dave Carr and two other blokes I'd never even met. I was remanded to Brixton prison and eventually spent a year there before being found not guilty at the Old Bailey. People I knew were in the protection game, demanding money with menaces, but it never appealed to me. I didn't want to go around robbing and hurting people – that's why I never got into blags. I always had cash, so the Old Bill must have assumed I was into protection. But all I'd ever done was take it off villains and people who could afford it and deserved to be conned. It was often easy money and there was no violence involved.

While I was in Brixton, I bumped into my Scottish pal Tam Rea. He was awaiting trial for a million-pound fraud and convinced he had nothing to worry about. He was right and was found not guilty at trial.

Being on remand in prison might sound the pits, but it was an occupational hazard for our game. Getting someone like me off the streets for a year was a big win for the police, even if the charges were eventually thrown out. It was a constant game of cat and mouse.

and then, his [illegible] by turning up [illegible] that [illegible] though Lenny had just [illegible] by [illegible] had pointed the door [illegible] little thing than the [illegible] the [illegible] for them [illegible] though he meant [illegible] days [illegible]

A few months later [illegible] was arrested and charged with demanding [illegible] Dave [illegible] and two other [illegible] having [illegible] before being [illegible] at the Old Bailey [illegible] protection [illegible] demanding money with [illegible] and [illegible] robbing and burning people [illegible] for the [illegible] I [illegible] had [illegible] protection [illegible] and people who could [illegible] and [illegible] was not [illegible] myself.

The [illegible] but [illegible] that [illegible] and [illegible] was [illegible] not quite [illegible]

[illegible] was [illegible] and [illegible] the [illegible]

CHAPTER SIXTEEN

'I SHOULD'VE GUESSED HE HAD NO INTENTION OF FIGHTING FAIR. AS WE GOT ON TO THE COBBLES HE PULLED A KNIFE FROM HIS COAT AND LUNGED AT ME. I SPUN ROUND AND CRACKED HIM ON THE JAW. IT WAS A PERFECT PUNCH AND HE WENT DOWN LIKE A SACK OF SHIT. BUT HE WAS A BIG BLOKE AND COULD CLEARLY TAKE SOME PUNISHMENT, AND HE PULLED HIMSELF UP, SHAKILY WAVING HIS BLADE IN FRONT OF HIM LIKE HE WAS CONDUCTING A BLEEDIN' ORCHESTRA OR SOMETHING. I PUT HIM BACK DOWN WITH A FLURRY OF PUNCHES, THEN KICKED THE KNIFE DOWN A DRAIN...'

DOG DAYS

I was hung over and feeling rough as a dog as I crossed Silvertown Way in Canning Town on my way home after a night on the tiles when I heard the roar of an engine and the screech of tyres. It was a Saturday morning and early, so I'd barely checked the road for traffic as I stepped off the pavement. Now out of the corner of my eye I caught sight of a black Mercedes speeding towards me, its wheels belching smoke as they spun wildly, seeking purchase on the wet road surface.

I had seconds to react and flung myself back towards the pavement as the car rocketed towards me. I was too late. Its front bumper clipped my legs, sending me flying on to the tarmac and rolling into the kerbstone, badly shaken and bruised. The Merc stopped up the road and then, with more screeching of tyres, performed a sharp U-turn and stopped, its engine revving ominously.

I dragged myself upright and, with hands that were bloodied and dirty, grabbed half a brick that was lying in the gutter and stumbled into the centre of the road ready to hurl my makeshift weapon through the windscreen.

'C'mon then, you fucker,' I screamed at the car in a blind rage.

The engine revved a couple of times then the car spun round and roared off in the opposite direction. I lurched to the side of the road and collapsed on the pavement. The windows had been darkened so I had no idea who was driving the car but they were undoubtedly trying to kill me. Had I not moved fast enough, the Merc would have hit me head on. At that speed I would have been dead.

Suddenly, I realised I was shaking with a combination of adrenalin and shock. My leather jacket was scuffed and muddied from the road. I managed to get home and into the shower. My legs were already bruising heavily and I was cut badly across my shoulders where I'd come down and rolled across the road.

After making myself a cup of tea, I sat down, turned on the telly for a mental massage, and tried to work out who could have wanted to kill me, or at the very least scare the crap out of me, with a stunt like that. Despite my line of work, cornering the gullible, the list was not a long one. I had never hidden from my enemies, deciding early in my career that lancing a boil quickly was better than letting it fester. Many good East End lives had been lost because petty rows or disagreements were allowed to escalate dangerously out of control. Consequently, I took my enemies as they came, often sorting problems without having to resort to violence, and life had been good for months.

Earlier that year, my old pal Richie Reynolds, who had been in Wayland prison with Danny Woollard and Reggie Kray, had asked me to visit him at his home in Harlow. We met and he told me he had a problem with the son-in-law of Levi Silks, the renowned gypsy fighter I'd fought and beaten at Yalding a couple of years previously. They'd fallen out over a deal gone sour and, knowing my contacts, Richie asked if I could intervene before things got out of hand. Danny Woollard was a good mate of Levi so we arranged a summit at the Cock Inn Hotel in a little Hertfordshire village called Sheering. An old mate of mine, Billy Bedford, was landlord so we all had a good day and there was no hint of aggravation. As ever, Levi was a gentleman and, thankfully, Richie's troubles were soon smoothed over.

On the way home, I stopped in at the British Lion pub in Stratford for a celebratory pint. It's not there any more, but in its day it was one of the East End's roughest boozers and a hotbed of villains. It was where the cops had snatched Jimmy Boyle on murder charges, while I stood gobsmacked at the bar.

The Lion had become famous for having one of the fattest pub dogs in London. The poor thing stood no chance, living as it did on a diet consisting of almost nothing but pork scratchings and half-eaten sarnies. Today, the mutt was struggling to beg any food from the punters. There was a new barmaid pulling pints and getting all the attention. She said her name was Janine. She was in her mid-thirties, blonde, gorgeous and posh too. Her accent alone got her noticed in the East End. I chatted her up and persuaded her to give me her number.

The next day I phoned her and within a week we were knocking about together. She was fantastic, a real tonic after Maureen and Janet, and we had a laugh together. She didn't care who I was or what I did. Nor was she enamoured of the East End. She'd been working at the Lion by chance because a friend owned it at the time. Her parents lived in Hampshire. They'd done well but Janine had never got on with them and they'd written her off. She'd come to London to be an actress but had never got beyond small parts. Now she was deciding what she wanted to do with the rest of her life. Before long I was hoping we might be spending it together. What a mug.

I was earning good money buying and selling knocked-off goods and enjoying life for the first time in months. I cut back on the drinking and womanising and even started to see myself settling down with Janine. Things were that good. I didn't realise it at the time but it couldn't last. I should've been suspicious when she admitted she wasn't called Janine. Her real name was Vicki Hodge. She was an actress, that much was true, but it took weeks and my near-death experience before she finally let me in on her secret life.

After my run-in with the Merc, I went to see Vicki, or Janine, as I'd got used to calling her, that evening at work. She didn't seem remotely shocked when I showed her my legs, now black and blue.

'Micky, I have a confession to make,' she told me. 'Before I was seeing you, there was another man I was with for about four years. I'm not seeing him now but when we first met I was still with him.'

I was fuming but I stayed outwardly calm. 'It's OK, Janine. I understand,' I replied. 'Who is this mug? Is he the one who tried to run me down?'

She looked guiltily at the floor and then replied: 'His name's John Bindon and he's an actor. He's very jealous. He's done this sort of thing before. He's a very violent man and he might try to kill you.'

He already has, love, I thought.

I needed to be alone to sort things out in my head. I told Vicki I'd call her in a couple of days when I'd worked out what to do. I got home and started drinking until I lost my rag and punched the wall in frustration. I had thought I loved Janine or Vicki or whoever she was, but she had deceived me and I was worried I couldn't trust her.

She could've got me killed or maimed. I wasn't blaming her for Bindon being an unstable psychopath, but she could at least have warned me he was in the frame and on the loose. Looking back, I was an idiot to lose my rag. I'd often had two or three women on the go and we were truly great together.

I knew Bindon by reputation only. He was an archetypal working-class boy made good, then made bad again, and his nickname was 'Biffo' because of his love of starting fights. Like me, he was the son of a merchant sailor and also like me he'd served time in borstal, after being caught by the cops with live ammunition. That was where our similarities ended. Unlike me, he was a bully and a crook, who had moved into extortion, running parts of West London before being 'discovered' in his early twenties in a pub by the film director Ken Loach.

In an era when working-class accents were never heard on the radio or TV, Bindon struck a nerve. He made his name as an actor in films such as *Poor Cow* and *Get Carter* and starred alongside Mick Jagger in *Performance*. But fame and fortune, including reputedly shagging Princess Margaret on Mustique, and dating Christine Keeler and Angela Barnett (who went on to marry David Bowie), couldn't keep him on the straight and narrow. He'd been unable to shake off his underworld connections and his love of the dark side. In a nutshell, he was a heavy drinker, womaniser, perpetual brawler and violent thug. The sort I knew well.

A couple of years earlier, Bindon had been involved in a fight with gangster John Darke outside the Ranelagh Yacht Club in Fulham, stabbing him nine times and leaving Darke mortally wounded before fleeing the scene. Bindon covered up his own wounds and ran to Dublin but gave himself up to the police. At his Old Bailey trial in 1979, the prosecution claimed he'd been paid £10,000 to kill Darke over a drug debt and the fight was a cover for his death. Bindon's own brief argued that Darke was killed in self-defence, claiming his client had been in fear of his life as he was being blackmailed about losing drug money and cocaine worth thousands of pounds. Despite having bragged to his cellmate about being a hitman while on remand, Bindon was acquitted of murder, in part thanks to the appearance of actor Bob Hoskins as a character witness.

Now he was a free man and after his acquittal clearly felt he was untouchable by the cops. I assumed I'd be hearing more from him now he'd failed to run me down.

About a week later, my relationship with Janine still unresolved, I was having a drink in the Britannia pub in Plaistow. It was smoke-filled and gloomy, just the way a proper boozer should be. A slash of light momentarily crossed the bar as someone walked in; it was Bindon and two other blokes. I recognised him straight off from the telly but he looked bigger and uglier in the flesh. He was well dressed and clearly monied, but he had a rough edge too. You could see why the camera loved him. The bar had been busy but my fellow drinkers, sensing trouble, their invisible East End antennae twitching, melted away and the barman found something else to do round the back as Bindon walked up to me.

'You're Micky Glückstad,' he told me.

'You should have been a policeman, not a fucking actor,' I replied. 'I'm having a quiet drink here. What do you want?'

'You know what this is about, Glückstad.'

'Try me,' I turned back to finish my drink to show I didn't give a fuck who he was.

'You've been messing about with my girl. I'm not having that.'

'Listen, Bindon,' I snarled, turning back to him and getting off my stool. 'It's a free country and Janine, er Vicki, is allowed to see who she wants. Even me. If you've got a problem with that then it's tough shit.'

He didn't flinch. I reckon he was half-cut on drugs and probably thought he was in a movie. Instead, he said: 'Let's settle this outside.'

You could sense the barman's relief as we trooped towards the door. Bindon and his mates followed me out. I should've guessed he had no intention of fighting fair. As we got on to the cobbles, he pulled a knife from his coat and lunged at me. I spun round and cracked him on the jaw. It was a perfect punch and he went down like a sack of shit. But he was a big bloke and could clearly take some punishment, and he pulled himself up, shakily waving his blade in front of him like he was conducting a bleedin' orchestra or something.

I put him back down with a flurry of punches, then kicked the knife down a drain. Without it, he was just another pathetic bully. I went at him hard and felled him like an oak. Now I turned on the chainsaw and worked his body with my fists and feet till he was out for the count. I kicked him in the head a couple of times to make sure he wasn't coming back at me then spat on him.

'You fucking slag. Stay away from me and Vicki, you little c**t, or I'll do you properly.'

I looked at his two mates, daring them to make a move, but they didn't want to know. They picked him up and stuffed him in the back of his black Merc – the car he'd tried to run me down in.

Before they drove off, I told them: 'It's finished between me and Vicki. She never told me about that c**t.'

A bloodstain was spreading over my trousers and shirt above my hip where Bindon had caught me with his knife. A friend drove me to A&E where I had 38 stitches. Someone had tipped off the police and they came to the hospital. I told them I'd been mugged. The two coppers knew I was lying but didn't care. As far as the Old Bill was concerned, Micky Glückstad could die in a gutter and it would be good riddance to bad rubbish. There's still a few cops working and many now retired who'll be popping the champagne corks the day I finally go.

After I got fixed up, I never heard from Vicki again. She left the British Lion soon afterwards and went back to Bindon. I missed her for a while but I got over it. Bindon starred in a couple more movies, including The Who's brilliant film about the Mods, *Quadrophenia*, then became a recluse, before eventually dying from either Aids or cancer depending on who tells the story. Either is a terrible way to go, but I have no doubt he got everything he deserved.

Al Capone was one of America's most notorious gangsters, up to his eyeballs in murder, extortion, bribery, prostitution, gambling and bootlegging. And what did he get sent down for? Tax evasion. When you get a reputation as a bad boy, the authorities will do anything to put you away. Absolutely anything. I know people who got away with murder then got jailed for unpaid parking tickets. Keep your nose clean or you risk losing your liberty over some poxy misdemeanour. Don't give the authorities any opportunity to get their claws into you.

If I'd followed my own advice, I'd have spent half as much time behind bars. Some chance. Billy Gibney was living in West Ham and had split with his latest girlfriend, so I went round to offer my sympathies. She'd been cheating on him – I should know, having slept with her behind his back when he was away – but he was cut up all the same. Billy had bought a brand-new Vauxhall Viva and it looked the dog's bollocks. Compared with today's cars, it was small, boxy and slow, but back in the day it was a beauty. It was a dark, stormy night and the wind was howling so Billy asked if I wanted to drive his car to the pub while he finished some business. I had no insurance, but what were the chances of being stopped?

The rain was lashing down when I jumped in the car, making it impossible to see through the windscreen. I wound down the side window and negotiated carefully down Billy's road. Cars were parked on either side, squeezing the road, so I slowed right down when I saw headlights coming towards me. It was a police Morris Minor with two coppers in it. As we inched past each other, one of the cops signalled me to pull over. Fuck knows why he'd decided to make my life difficult but I was buggered if I was going to give him the satisfaction. Chucking the car into first, I floored it and screeched off with the tyres spinning. I shot off down the road, turned left then left again, before pulling over in a side street and jumping out. It was still pissing it down as I walked back to Billy's flat, shoulders hunched against the rain.

As I strolled up to the gate, a police car pulled up. Unseen by the Old Bill, I dropped the car keys in the hedge.

'You're nicked,' said the younger cop, reaching to grab my shoulder.

Before he touched me, I'd punched him in the face, knocking him to the ground. Within seconds, more police were pulling up and, before I could make a dash for it, I was handcuffed and being beaten by the side of the road. The copper I'd knocked out took particular delight in hammering my arms, legs and body with his truncheon until I was yelling in agony. Afterwards, they hustled me into a van and took me to Forest Gate police station where I was charged with grievous bodily harm on a police officer.

Locked up overnight, I appeared black and blue in front of West Ham magistrates in Stratford the next morning and was bailed to appear before Snaresbrook Crown Court, in Wanstead, a month later because assaulting a police officer was a serious charge. When asked about my injuries, the cops told the court I'd resisted arrest – which was partly true, I suppose.

Back in the day, the police had carte blanche to do what they saw fit. It was common to get a good kicking in the cells whether you were guilty or not. If you were there, so it went, you must've done something and you should take it like a man.

As I walked out of court, one of the coppers hissed at me: 'You're looking at five years for this, Glückstad, you c**t.'

When it came to court, neither copper could be sure I'd been behind the wheel of the car they'd tried to pull over. The rain had made it impossible to be certain and my barrister made mincemeat out of them. Regarding the assault, the officer I'd smacked spun a sob story to the court claiming I'd nearly broken his jaw and he'd been off work since then.

When my turn came, I told the judge and jury I'd been on my way to see a friend when I'd been jumped by two police officers in the dark. One of them raised his fist and, fearing I was going to be smacked, I put my hands up in self-defence. In doing so, I had pushed the copper's fist back into his face, your honour, and he had knocked himself out. As a former promising amateur boxer, who had worked as a sparring partner twice a week with some of the biggest names in the business, my reactions were quicker than a normal man's.

I could hear titters coming from the jury bench so I carried on. I was very sorry the officer had been forced to take four weeks off work but I was a law-abiding man going about his business.

The cops' faces were a sight to behold as I was found not guilty on all charges. The judge and jury clearly believed my story. I practically believed it myself by the time I'd finished.

Afterwards, with Arnie Fouste and Billy, I went for a celebratory drink. Arnie stuck the jukebox on – playing 'The Great Pretender'.

* * *

About this time, a good friend of mine was running a club called the Galleons in Custom House, East London. Peter Morris was a proper gentleman. A big bloke who had been a formidable professional boxer but never a bully. We'd known each other for years and I trusted him like a brother.

I was drinking with him one afternoon after helping Danny Woollard deliver some barrels of beer to his club. A session developed and Peter and another pal, Micky O'Shea, wanted to carry on drinking at another pub. I cried off. I'd been on the sauce for a couple of days already and needed a break.

After getting home and sobering up, I changed my mind. I jumped in a cab to the Telegraph, where Peter and Micky had been headed. It was a scene of complete chaos by the time I arrived. There were police everywhere and forensic experts in boiler suits crawling around on their knees. Spotting someone I knew, I asked what was going on. It was Peter. He was dead. He'd got into a fight and been shot and hit over the head with a machete. I was dumbstruck. It was yet another close friend who would not live to the comfortable old age he deserved.

The grapevine was soon buzzing with details of the murder.

They were truly horrifying, even by the sometimes appalling standards of East End violence. Peter had been shot but not killed then smashed across the skull with some kind of machete or cleaver. It had taken the top of his skull and scalp clean off, killing him instantly through massive loss of blood and brain damage. The killers had fled the scene and there were no witnesses. I was reeling when the police arrived at my door the next day. They knew I had been drinking with Peter earlier in the day and accused me of sending him to the Telegraph to sort out a rival. I laughed at that. If someone needed sorting, they knew I'd be only too happy to do them myself.

I spent 48 hours in custody answering their questions. For once the code of conduct that says a villain should never answer the police with anything other than a firm 'no comment' meant nothing to me. If there was anything I could do to help catch Peter's killers, I would do it. I told the police everything I could remember about the day, what Peter had said and where he was going. It was mystifying. He had no enemies and no one bore him a grudge. Finally, the Old Bill realised I was properly cut up about his death and had not been involved.

They released me without charge and carried on their enquiries elsewhere.

When I got home, I broke down and cried. Of all the friends I lost over the years, Peter's death seemed the most senseless. To this day, no one has taken the rap for his murder, which is a fucking liberty. I'd love to know who was responsible and I hope they get their just deserts in time.

CHAPTER SEVENTEEN

'I'D NEVER FANCIED MYSELF FOR BREAKING AND ENTERING BUT PERHAPS THERE WAS SOMETHING IN IT AFTER ALL. MENTALLY TOTTING UP THE NIGHT'S PROFIT, THIS COULD TURN OUT TO BE THE EASIEST MONEY I'D EVER MADE, EVEN WHEN I'D LOOKED AFTER MY SNOUTS. SO WENT MY TRAIN OF THOUGHT AS I MOTORED ACROSS LONDON, DRIVING THE LORRY AND ITS LUCRATIVE LOAD TO THE SLAUGHTER...'

BREAKING AND ENTERING

'Big' Paul Foley was on the phone. 'Micky, I've taken over running Mooro's nightclub in Stratford,' he told me. 'It used to be a trouble pub but it's running OK now and I want to keep it that way.'

Everyone thought the club was owned by England and West Ham legend Bobby Moore, but in fact a couple of likely lads called the Quill brothers were behind it. They were old-school businessmen who kept a low profile and their heads down. For three months, I stood at the bar in Mooro's and, aside from a couple of minor dust-ups, kept the peace. Big Paul was happy, the Quills were happy, the alcohol was flowing and the tills were ringing.

I was happy enough sitting at my usual table by the door of an evening, keeping a close eye on things. I rarely had to get up and the waitresses made sure I was well refreshed. It was too good to last. The police heard I was on Mooro's payroll and told the Quills to get rid of me or they'd come down on the place like a ton of bricks. It was no contest. So even though I'd kept the club clean the cops wanted rid. I didn't bear the Quills any ill will. It was just business, and they bunged me a few quid to leave. It had been a nice gig, but now I was back to square one.

Billy Neal was best man at my wedding as well as being my brother-in-law, having married my sister Eileen, but we were always friends even before we were relatives. So there was a lot of trust there. Billy knew I was down in the dumps and looking for a job so he introduced me to a drinking mate of his, a night watchman who'd recently been given the sack by the Dagenham delivery company he worked for. Now he was looking for a payday and thought he had the information to justify one.

He told us the lorries were often left loaded at night so they could be sent off early from the warehouse before the rush hour. They carried all sorts, from TVs to computers to kitchen appliances, all high-end gear with a good resale value if you knew the right person to fence them to. The best thing was, the keys to all 12 vehicles had to be kept in a cabin by the yard by law so they could be moved if there was a fire. The bloke told us: 'The alarm system is a joke. It's a dummy. You can get under or over the gate. There are no cameras and no guards now they've got rid of me.'

It sounded like a dream job. Billy was on the straight and narrow but I reckoned I could carry this one on my own.

The next day, I took a quiet look at the yard. As promised, the gate looked like it would struggle to stop a shopping trolley and the parking area was well hidden from the road. Peering round the corner I clocked the security cabin. It was a prefab with paper-thin walls and a battered old door. It clearly wouldn't present much of an obstacle.

I'd been burned before when a similar 'easy' job landed me in prison for a year as part of a Flying Squad sting, so I wasn't taking any chances. I went for a drink then hung around across the street at a bus stop waiting for the drivers to clock off. Come 6pm, the lorries were back in the pound and the drivers had left. The last bloke, presumably the firm's manager, locked the gate behind him and with barely a glance around walked off whistling. I hadn't seen a copper all day and nothing was ringing alarm bells. Fuck it. I'd risk it. I went to the pub to let things quieten down and planned to be back at 8pm. I didn't want to make it too late or someone might get suspicious about a delivery lorry on the road after hours.

I'd brought leather gloves and a woollen hat, which I pulled low over my face to make it difficult to identify me if I got spotted. It was dark and cold and there was no one around when I returned. The gate had buckled and the bottom wasn't flush with the ground. I reckoned I could get under it if I pushed hard. With a final glance around I was on the floor and under the gate in seconds. After picking myself up, I hugged the shadows by the wall and waited. Not a sound.

Trying to stick to the shadows, I made my way cautiously to the security hut, glancing in the window to check it was empty. No one was home. Billy's snout had been spot on. The door splintered under my shoulder and I was inside. My torch quickly illuminated the keys, carefully labelled and hanging in a rack on the wall. I chose the lorry nearest the gate. The watchman reckoned that was the one most likely to be holding goods overnight. Without further ado, I had a quick look in the back. It was packed full of crates of microwave ovens. My luck was in. They were the latest must-have gadget for the hard-pressed housewife and would fetch a tidy sum on the black market. I just had to get the gate open and the lorry out before anyone clocked me.

I was breathing hard with the tension and trying to keep as quiet as possible as I returned to the security office. The watchman had said there might be a spare gate key in a drawer. Otherwise, I'd have to try to break the padlock and chain somehow. As luck would have it, the key was there, neatly labelled and everything.

It went like a dream. I opened the gate, had a quick look around then reversed the lorry out of the yard, before locking the gate behind me and chucking the key down a nearby drain. For a moment I was tempted to call some mates to fill their boots but I quickly discarded the idea. Getting greedy had cost me my freedom on more than one occasion. This was a perfect job. Why ruin it by bringing others in on it?

Within minutes, I was out on the A13 heading for the motorway. I'd had a quiet chat that afternoon with a bloke I knew in Croydon who was expecting me, should the job be a good 'un. I'd never fancied myself for breaking and entering but perhaps there was something in it after all. Mentally totting up the night's profit, this could turn out to be the easiest money I'd ever made, even when I'd looked after my snouts. So went my train of thought as I motored across London, driving the lorry and its lucrative load to the slaughter. My hopes were dashed when we got the lorry into my mate's lock-up and opened the back to retrieve the boxes.

Fuck me backwards. The crates were only empty! Sometimes you just had to laugh at the stupidity of life.

It was all going wrong until a few weeks later, out of the blue, I was challenged to a prizefight by Harry 'The Buck' Starbuck, a gypsy from Charlton whose family had stakes in a number of East London boozers. He had a tasty reputation for knocking out his opponents and was being looked after by Eddie Richardson, a serious South London face who had aspired to rival the Krays with his brother Charlie in the late sixties.

The bout was billed as a night of professional boxing at the Downham Tavern in Lewisham with seven fights in total. We were topping the bill and tickets were going like hot cakes. The Buck was using the fight as a warm-up for taking on Roy Shaw, who I'd already beaten, and we were due to contest eight two-minute rounds on a winner-takes-all basis. It was good business. I sold 100 tickets no bother, then I spent the takings, thinking I'd pay the promoters back with my winnings.

With two weeks to go before the fight, The Buck pulled out. I reckon he bottled it because he knew he'd lose. In his book, *The Guv'nor*, Lenny McLean claimed Richardson turned down

10 grand and a challenge to fight Starbuck, telling him: 'If you come over here you'll do him, I know you will, then we're 10 grand out and we've lost our pension.' I reckon that was about the long and the short of it with me. Starbuck's people had checked me out and reckoned, on reflection, I was more trouble than it was worth. Anyway, I was stuck, owing 100 punters their money and no bout in the offing. Danny Woollard came round to see what I was going to do.

'I might as well be hung for a sheep as a lamb,' I told Danny. 'Come back tomorrow and we'll get to work.'

The next day Danny pulled up in his motor and I got in, carrying a briefcase. Inside were another 1,000 tickets to the bout.

'Let's go to work,' I said.

We spent six days driving all over London flogging the tickets and we sold the lot. The ringside seats were going for £8 each so it was a decent haul.

On the night, there were coachloads of punters turning up and no main event. No one ever got their money back and I might not have fought on the night but I had one or two punch-ups over the no-show. It was worth it – I had money in my pocket again and was riding high on it.

Back home there was a letter and a visiting order from another old East End friend, Johnny West, who was on remand at Winchester prison for something or other. Billy Gibney agreed to come along for the ride that weekend. It was a hot day and we pulled up at a petrol station in Guildford to grab a couple of cans of drink.

I walked into the shop but there was no one around. Looking over to the cash till I could hardly believe my eyes – it was open and full of money. I was mentally totting it up – a tidy sum that would be worth a punt on in the days before everything was covered by CCTV cameras. Robbery's no job for the camera shy these days, but then, if the cops didn't have a witness, they were screwed.

'Keep an eye open, Bill,' I muttered, reaching over the counter to grab a wad of tenners. Just as I was taking the money, the manager walked in from a door behind the counter. He must've been taking a leak. Shit. I was caught red-handed.

Very slowly, so as not to panic him, I put the money down on the counter and said to the bloke: 'Keep your mouth shut, mate, and you won't get hurt. I'm putting the cash down here. It's all there. You count it.'

The manager had gone as white as a sheet and didn't say a word as I walked out, though I could see him reaching for the phone and grabbing the pile of cash as I left. Bill was standing open-mouthed outside the door, having seen everything through the glass.

'Come on, mate. Let's get going,' I said.

We never made it to Winchester nick to see Johnny. That would have to wait, though I thought for a moment we might be joining him after all. Half a dozen police cars and vans surrounded us before we'd even left Guildford. We were arrested, handcuffed and locked up for the rest of the weekend at Guildford police station, charged with attempted robbery.

It was inevitable. Plain old-fashioned bad luck. But we hadn't actually stolen anything so I was confident we'd walk free when the beak arrived on Monday morning. What could we have done other than walk away? I hadn't been planning on a career in robbery; it wasn't my style and the bloke had seen us. Neither was I planning on branching into murder, so I'd been out of options.

Up before the local magistrates on Monday morning, we both pleaded guilty, thinking we'd be fined and sent home. Not so. Instead, we were remanded for a week to Wandsworth prison, while our homes were turned over by the Flying Squad. They found nothing at my place but came up with a sawn-off shotgun at Billy's. I couldn't complain too much – I'd given the bloody thing to him. But the cops must've been cracking open the champagne. Suddenly we were facing serious charges. We were carted back to Guildford magistrates charged with firearms offences. Unbeknown to us, two armed robbers had been blagging petrol stations and stores in the Guildford area for the past two months using a sawn-off, and the police, never the world's most original thinkers, were now convinced they had their men.

We were remanded again to appear before Guildford Crown Court on charges of armed robbery and sent to Wandsworth prison. We were looking down the barrel of a 10-year sentence if found guilty. I could barely look Billy in the eye. I'd been a bloody mug for reaching for that cash. I remembered an old adage my dad liked to repeat: 'If something looks too good to be true, it probably bloody is.' One thing is for sure; it's always the easy money that will get you in the end.

Thankfully, lady luck, who had been so sorely missed, finally came good for us after seven weeks inside. The real armed robbers were caught at another petrol station and fingered for all the jobs up until then. Then, in court, the cops had to admit there was no firing pin in the sawn-off. As luck would have it, I'd removed it before giving Bill the gun. I told the court I'd bought the gun as a gift for him to put on his wall. It was only for show. The firearms charges were dropped after three days of legal arguments and the judge decided to give us a break by not sending us to prison. The petrol-station manager confirmed we'd not actually taken a penny and the judge put the whole incident down to foolish high jinks, much to the annoyance of the local Old Bill. We were heavily fined, freed from the dock and told in no uncertain terms never to return to Guildford. We left without looking back.

The story of my life has been wrong place, wrong time. Another incident happened when I was drinking with a Scottish bloke I knew called Tam Rea in the Lord Stanley pub in Plaistow. Tam was about as wide as a lorry, buying and selling everything and usually turning a good profit. As I was later to discover, he'd branched out into drugs and was making tidy money dealing.

If I'd known, I'd have run a mile. The last thing I needed now was a drugs bust. I never got mixed up in drugs, never took them and never needed to. Alcohol was my drug of choice and I wasn't keen on anything harder. That was Tam's business, though. I might not have agreed but it was his fat to fry. Having said that, I didn't want to get fried with it, but it's easy to be wise after the event.

Tam was heading to another pub and asked if I fancied keeping him company. I didn't mind, and we ended up in Canning Town. Tam was quickly away into a corner with a bloke called Danny Woods, a local hard man and prizefighter, and two or three of his mates.

I had no idea what they were up to and was having a drink at the bar when up pops Tam. 'C'mon, Micky, let's shoot,' he said, grabbing my arm and hustling me out of the pub.

'What's going on?' I asked.

'I've just sold them a load of dodgy coke. There's more baby milk formula in it than drugs,' he laughed.

I realised then he was off his head and bundled him towards a waiting taxi. The night was rapidly going tits up and I had no desire to get caught up in trouble. As usual, I didn't have a choice. Before we could jump in the cab, Woods and his mates came charging out of the pub having realised they had been ripped off.

They were furious and set about Tam before I could intervene to stop them. He was on the ground unconscious in seconds. Now I'd have to get involved. Placing myself between Tam, who appeared to be alive but bleeding heavily from his head, and his angry erstwhile customers, I snarled: 'How about you and me, Woods? Here on the cobbles, toe to toe. Just the two of us.'

I had a reputation but Woods was a tasty fighter too. He wasn't going to waste time. Without saying a word he swung at me, a sweeping roundhouse to the head. If it had caught me I'd have been down and out. As a veteran pub brawler, I was ready for him and too quick. I blocked his fist and pulled him off balance, using his own weight against him and dragging him on to a left hook.

It was a heavy punch and he took the full force to the head. As he went down, one of his pals squirted liquid ammonia in my face. The pain was excruciating. Tears were pouring from my eyes and I was struggling to see. Another of the thugs leaned in and calmly stabbed me in the chest. These boys were playing for keeps. I couldn't believe it. Tam was not worth getting murdered for.

Woods was coming up. I could see well enough to kick him in the head, sending him flying on to the road again. His mates had legged it back into the pub. I followed them, bellowing with anger and pain.

Charging over to the bar, I kicked the counter up, went behind the bar and stuck my face under the tap used to clean glasses. The relief was immediate. Now where were those little c**ts? The governor was holding his hands up. 'C'mon, Micky, we don't want any trouble with you here,' he said.

'I'll do the lot of them,' I swore. 'Where are they?'

'They've done a runner, Micky. They're long gone.'

He was right. It was just a few old-age pensioners and some office girls. Outside, Tam was getting unsteadily to his feet. I dragged him into the cab. Back home, I washed my eyes out again and examined my chest. The blade had gone in under my collarbone, thankfully missing any vital organs. It wasn't a deep wound and had stopped bleeding so I washed it out and taped it up before chucking back some painkillers.

A few days later, it went round Canning Town that Woods and his mates were being sorted out. No one wanted any trouble with Micky Glückstad and I was happy to let it go. The last thing I needed was more bother with the police.

A few months later, Danny Woods, who had changed his

surname to Reece for some reason, was sent down for conspiring with the 'Black Widow' Linda Calvey to murder her lover Ronnie Cook for £10,000. Typically, he bottled it, leaving Calvey to shoot Cook as her former lover begged for his life on his hands and knees.

CHAPTER EIGHTEEN

'SUDDENLY I WAS IN MY ELEMENT AND MY TIREDNESS DISAPPEARED. I WAS BUZZING AT THE THOUGHT OF A GOOD CON, THE ADRENALIN PUMPING... THIS BLOKE WAS RIPE TO BE RIPPED OFF BIG TIME. I LOOKED AROUND AND TOOK A DEEP BREATH...'

THE CON IS BACK ON

I was having a hell of a run of bad luck. I'd driven up to Manchester to see an old pal I'd been locked up with years before and my car had broken down, so I'd dumped it and jumped on the train back to London. Then the train broke down, and the heating on the reserve train went tits up, so I arrived back in Euston late, cold, in a stinking mood, and with just £10 and my car keys in my pocket. I was going to dump the keys but for some reason I didn't. They were to prove invaluable.

A few weeks before, I'd been out with my old friend Michael Collins. Mike had always had his head screwed on. Out of all the old gang at Whitehall School in Forest Gate he had looked most likely to clean up financially and he'd done well for himself since I'd knocked him off his perch as school tough with the help of Mr Vicks. He owned a big house and a thriving car dealership out in Canning Town. He was doing well and kept nine classic cars he had collected in a special garage.

When I was short of dough, he'd sometimes take me on as a salesman, working on commission. Given my gift of the gab, I was a natural and could do a car a week easily. It wasn't completely legit; Mike was paying me cash in hand for my work, but it was good money and I liked working for him. It wasn't exactly a nine-to-five job – that's a prison sentence in itself – but it suited me nicely.

That Friday night we went out to celebrate another sale and got steaming drunk. It was getting late and Mike wanted to carry on at a nightclub in Stratford where he knew the governor, but I was knackered for once and cried off, so I left my own car outside Mike's house and jumped in a cab, waving him goodbye. It was the last time I saw my old friend alive. Mike went on to the club where he was ambushed outside. He had a glass of acid thrown in his face before being stabbed to death by two men. It was a cowardly and brutal attack on a good man who deserved better.

Someone told the police Mike had been demanding protection money from the club, and I was his partner. The next morning, I heard the news when I went to pick up my car. Mike's missus was in a terrible state and I tried to console her.

'Micky, why has this happened?' she sobbed.

For once, I didn't have an answer. I put my arms round her and hugged her as tight as I could. It was a terrible shock to everyone who knew Mike and a completely senseless waste of a life. He had been a hard man, but he was honest and had done nothing to provoke this attack, as far as we knew. Mike's wife told me the police wanted to talk to me as I was the last person to see him before he went to the club.

As I left, I promised: 'If we find out who was responsible for this, the police won't be needed.'

She just shook her head and walked back inside.

That afternoon, I walked into Canning Town nick and asked to speak to the officer in charge of the case. As usual, I was the prime suspect for the tragedy. The copper told me: 'We suspect you sent Mr Collins to the club to demand protection. His murder is on your conscience.'

Gritting my teeth, I said: 'Show me your evidence.'

They couldn't because there wasn't any. It was laughable, or it would've been if it didn't involve the death of my oldest friend. As far as the Old Bill was concerned, I was now a target criminal, someone they wanted off the streets for good. But they had nothing on me, so I walked out a free man.

It was another sad episode for our gang from Whitehall School. We never got to the bottom of Mike's death, and it still haunts me. There were times afterwards when I thought about jacking in life on the cobbles and going straight, though I doubt Uri Geller could have reformed me at that point. A criminal record is poison to an employer and I didn't have any qualifications to my name other than a quick wit. Instead, after Mike's funeral, I had gone to Manchester for a few weeks to try to clear my head.

Now I was back in town with a tenner to my name and no idea what I was going to do next. When the going gets tough, the tough go for a drink. So I strolled down the Euston Road to a lively backstreet bar I knew in King's Cross. It attracted a mixed crowd of faces, railwaymen and labourers, and I thought I might meet some mates and drum up business. I walked into the pub and I was halfway across the smoke-filled room to the bar when, out of the blue, a big Irish fella came up to me, reaching out a huge hand to shake mine.

'Hi, Terry,' he said. 'It is Terry, ain't it?'

What the hell, I thought. 'Sure, it's Terry. How are you?'

He leaned towards me and growled in my ear: 'I've got the money on me. Have you got the guns?'

I looked around. I had two thoughts: the first was that this must be some kind of a wind-up. I didn't know this bloke from Adam, but maybe someone had recognised me and was pulling my leg. He seemed legit, if stupid, though. The second thought came quickly: how could I get his money off him and get the hell out of here before the real Terry walked in? Suddenly I was in my element and my tiredness disappeared. I was buzzing at the thought of a good con, the adrenalin pumping. There is nothing more exciting than pitting your wits against another human being in a high-stakes game like this. And this bloke was ripe to be ripped off big time. I looked around and took a deep breath.

'Right, mate, how many of you are there?' I asked.

'Six of us,' he replied. 'I'm…'

'Don't tell me,' I interrupted, looking round again. 'I don't wanna know. OK, just you and one other come with me. The merchandise isn't here. Have you got transport?'

'Yes,' he said.

'Right, follow me.'

I walked out of the pub, followed by the big Irishman and his mate, a sneaky-looking ginger bloke. They had an old 12-seater navvy's van parked up the road. We jumped in, the Irishman's mate driving, and I directed them up the Pentonville Road towards Islington while I tried to get my horses in line.

As the van pulled away, I remembered an all-night lorry park and nearby pub in Clerkenwell, so I pointed them in the right direction and sat back thinking hard.

Five minutes later, we pulled up outside the boozer and I went in, the two blokes trotting after me. Using my last tenner, I ordered three pints and sunk half of mine in one. Right. This was it. The confidence game was on.

'Okay,' I said, 'money first, then I'll take you to the guns.'

'That wasn't the deal,' scowled the Irishman. 'We've got two envelopes here. Half now and half when we pick up the goods and check them over. Six grand total if everything's as agreed.'

'OK, that's fair to me,' I replied. 'You bring half and come with me and your mate waits here with the rest of the cash to complete the deal. The cargo is five minutes from here in a van. Any funny business and I'm gone.'

He nodded to his mate and followed me out of the pub and round the corner towards the lorry park. It was busy, thankfully, and I spotted a battered old Luton van parked up at the end of a row about 100 yards away. I took my old car keys out of my jacket and held them up for him to see.

'OK, mate, here's the keys, where's the envelope?' I asked.

The Irishman handed me a crumpled brown envelope. I fingered the corner of it and saw a wad of notes inside. My heart was pounding but outwardly I was calm.

'You think I want to rob you?' he asked, smiling.

'Here you go,' I said, chucking him the keys. 'The guns are in the back of that Luton. I'm going to go and finish my pint with your mate. See you in the boozer when you've checked them out. You can keep the van to transport them in but make sure you get rid of it properly afterwards.'

He nodded and set off towards the van. I turned and strolled back round the corner as casually as I could, then when I was out of sight ran back to the road. I had no intention of going back into the pub. I hailed a passing black cab and jumped in, telling the driver to take me back to the East End. I had no idea who I'd just tangled with, the IRA possibly, or a bunch of incompetent wannabe blaggers. I would never know, and didn't care. As we arrived in Shoreditch, I opened the envelope to pay the fare and laughed out loud. In between the tenners was a stack of newspaper nicely cut up to resemble a bundle of notes. So, the Irish firm had been going to rip off Terry, whoever the hell he was. Well, I'd saved them the trouble. But, despite their deceit, it was still a very tidy sum. I was £2,500 in profit and back on my feet.

The next day, I gave Mum and Dad a few quid for a holiday and bought myself a new car, a second-hand Bentley, cheap off a mate. When people asked about it, I told them I'd traded it for the keys to my old car.

My run of good luck continued. A few weeks later, Billy Gibney told me about a jeweller's shop in Holloway that was ripe for a job. The back door was never locked and the key to the safe was hung in plain view on the wall. We checked it out and it seemed kosher. Bill's informant thought there should be 20 grand's worth of gear in the safe on any given day so it was worth the risk, and we reckoned we could be in and out without anyone noticing. We certainly wouldn't be going in tooled up. That wasn't my style. This would be a case of softly, softly, catchee monkey. On the day, Bill stayed round the front, keeping watch, as I went round the back.

We'd taken the precaution of employing a very pretty ex-girlfriend of Billy's. Posing as a customer, she soon had most of the staff and the manager clucking over her as she tried on various bits and pieces of jewellery. We hoped this would keep the staff out of the back but I was seriously tense and, pulling a balaclava down over my face, I opened the door. The back office was empty, the door to the shop closed. I could barely believe it. On the wall, as promised, was the key to a big green Chubb safe sitting in the corner. I slipped it off its hook and tiptoed over to the safe. I was as nervous as I'd ever been. At any moment someone could walk in and I'd be done. The key slipped into the lock and turned silently. The door swung open.

Inside was an Aladdin's cave. There were four or five shelves. On the top two were a number of velvet jewellers' bags. I grabbed them one by one, stuffing them into the satchel I'd brought with me. There were boxes as well, but I left those. It wouldn't pay to be greedy when the clock was ticking. I quickly closed the safe and locked it, sticking the key back on its hook, and was out the door. The whole job had taken less than three minutes. It had gone like clockwork.

Pulling the balaclava off my head and stuffing it in my bag, I came out of the side street, nodded to Bill, who was loitering at a nearby bus stop, and strolled casually down the road. Later, we realised we had struck gold. In the bags was at least 100 grand's worth of diamonds, waiting to be inset in engagement or wedding rings. Even when we'd bunged Billy's snout handsomely for his information, and given his ex a nice little drink for playing her part, we were seriously quids in.

It took a couple of days for the story to break but the papers called it one of the biggest jewel heists in British history. The cops didn't have a clue. I always thought of this sort of crime as victimless; no one lost out. The insurers paid out for the missing stones, the newspapers got excited and sold loads of copies off the back of their manufactured outrage, the police ran around and shook up the local underworld, and the profits went back into the economy. Everyone won and it added a bit of excitement to everyday life.

We let the fuss die down then fenced the stones through a close friend and split the remaining money 50–50. Billy bought a house in East Ham and I sent Mum and Dad away for another holiday to Norway. Then we went out to celebrate. It was a sunny day in London, the sort of weather that always makes me wish I'd retired to Spain, far from the reach of Scotland Yard. If only. The two of us got plastered and ended up in a Chinese restaurant somewhere in Hoxton.

The East End had been changing in recent years. A lot of the old faces had been put away and the Krays were a distant memory. Immigration had transformed many of our old haunts and the new communities brought their own customs, and their own criminals. I had nothing against immigrants taking jobs – I knew they weren't for me. But I didn't like the thought of their gangs muscling in on our business. I reckon we fell foul of the so-called Triads that night. What started as a quiet meal ended up in a proper punch-up with Billy and myself on one side against at least 12 Chinese blokes. I can't even remember how it started now. But it ended with almost all of us in hospital, including Billy and me. I'd been hit with a cleaver across my head and needed stitches. Billy had also taken a beating, but we'd given a good account of ourselves too. When the police came asking, there were no witnesses.

When we got out of hospital, I invested in a scrap yard and put the rest of the diamond money into a printing business. The front was an upholsterer's, which was totally legit and owned by a Bangladeshi businessman. In the back room, which I'd rented cash in hand from him, I had two presses and two expert printers knocking out shady five-pound notes. The first ones that came off the presses didn't look right, but they kept working until we had it nailed. They were perfect. This was the big one.

Then, a month later, someone squealed and the Fraud Squad raided the firm. Both the printers got nicked and everything was impounded. They never let on that I was the backer and they got three years apiece. I made sure they were well looked after when they came out but I lost a lot of cash. If we had got those fivers out on to the black market, I reckon the Bank of England would have had to withdraw the whole lot from circulation. They were that good.

With the remainder of my money, I rented a big shop in Stratford and got some arcade machines and one-armed bandits in to open an amusement arcade, one of the first in London with Space Invaders. It was easy money and I was doing well until the Old Bill took an interest four weeks later. One of the local bigwigs walked in.

'Is this your shop, Glückstad?' he asked.

'No, mate. I'm just minding it for a friend,' I replied.

'We'll be watching you closely,' he said, and stalked out.

The rent book was in someone else's name so I didn't think they would bother me again but the police have a long collective memory and I was still top of their list.

They were worse than any protection racket. After that, they came back every week, scaring off the customers and trying to put me out of business until I gave up. I got a friend to come in as a partner and we built the business until there were 18 machines, a little café and some staff. Then the Old Bill put the taxman on to us and I told my mate I was pulling out. It was too much like hard work. He gave me a few pounds to keep the shop on and I was back on the lookout.

Soon afterwards, I was in the West End having a bit of a scout about and looking for ideas when I noticed a magazine advert for escorts. At that time, the vice trade was concentrated in Soho and the Vice Squad was always turning over clip joints and red-light flats to keep the locals in line. This could be easy money out in the sticks where it would attract less attention. I went to see Johnny Neal at his stonemason's shop in Leytonstone. He had a mate up the road with a shop and an empty three-bedroomed flat above it. I rented the flat, had it decorated and put a couple of phone lines in. Then I printed business cards advertising a new massage parlour and got a couple of likely lads on board as my frontmen and muscle. They would run the joint and make sure none of the customers got out of hand.

Next we recruited girls who wanted to work. Arnie Fouste knew plenty of girls on the game and four or five came on board with the promise of a proper share of the profits and protection from violent punters. It was all set. Then my two new business associates carried out a raid at a Stratford jewellers. They forced the owner on to his knees then blew his brains out. It was a cold-blooded execution. I don't know what possessed them but they were bang out of order. The jeweller had a family and there was no need for that sort of extreme violence and bloodletting. The next day, I arrived at the flat and was arrested by armed police. They dragged me from my car and handcuffed me. I was taken to West Ham police station where the cops accused me of funding the raid and supplying the shotgun used to murder the jeweller.

While I was being questioned, they ripped the flat apart looking for evidence. It was clean but they tore up the carpets, pulled out all the light fittings and even ripped out the bathroom. It was a write-off.

I told the cops I had nothing to do with the robbery. They didn't believe me but they had to release me. When the case came to court, my two former associates, who'd been nicked a couple of days after the killing, got 12 and 14 years apiece. They deserved every minute. My short foray into pimping was over before it began.

CHAPTER NINETEEN

'THE DAYS WHEN A GRUDGE COULD BE SETTLED ON THE COBBLES WERE NEARING AN END. WANNABE GANGSTERS WERE GETTING TOOLED UP TO GO TO THE SHOPS FOR A PINT OF MILK. SOME OF THE OLDER FACES USED THIS AS AN EXCUSE TO ARM THEMSELVES MORE HEAVILY BUT I DIDN'T LIKE IT ONE BIT. IF I'D LEARNED ONE THING, IT WAS THAT VIOLENCE BEGETS VIOLENCE...'

DUCKING AND DIVING

Inspired by the great Scottish boxer Ken Buchanan, who had all his televised fights taped and would organise showings for his pals, Danny Woollard and myself got our hands on tapes of some of the greatest bare-knuckle fighters from Roy Shaw's mate Joe Carrington, who had become a promoter. We had Shawy himself, Lenny McLean, Donny Adams and many others and I got them copied on to one tape. Then we organised a night of prizefighting at the Church Elm pub in Dagenham. An old mate of mine, Frank Jackson, was governor there. We agreed to charge a £5 entrance fee, then we hired a big screen and a projector and put posters up. Frank would take the bar money and we'd keep the cash from the door.

We had an amazing response and, on the night, nearly 350 people crammed into the pub to watch the fights. We kept everyone waiting as long as we could so Frank could take a few quid at the bar, then, about 9pm, we dimmed the lights for the main performance. There was a real air of expectancy; many of the punters had never seen a real unlicensed boxing match. The first fight on the tape was Roy Shaw versus 'Mad Dog' Mullins and the punters were lapping it up. It looked fantastic on the big screen and the atmosphere was electric.

Then, suddenly, about halfway through the fight, the tape went fuzzy and there was a burst of a familiar theme tune... 'Daaa-da-da-daa-da-da...'. Fuck me. It was *Coronation Street*. I'd left the video in the pub the night before and Frank's wife had accidentally taped over it. She'd left it running and come downstairs to serve customers and all the fights had been replaced by the previous night's TV. It was a disaster. The crowd was shouting and hollering for their money back. I stood up to try to calm things down and said I'd go and get a copy. Then Danny and I left as fast as we could. There was no copy.

No one got their money back because we'd already spent it. Someone nicked the projector and screen but we'd hired them under a fake name so that didn't bother us. Big Frank was OK about it. He'd made a pile on the bar. Later, he told us some of his customers were looking for us for their money back or revenge. But they couldn't have looked very hard because I never heard any more about it. It was very embarrassing at the time but we earned a nice little pot from it.

A friend of mine was working on the door at Stringfellows club in Covent Garden and invited me to come and have a few drinks. Stringy, as everyone knew him, did a great job of promoting his place and it was the hottest ticket in town. As I was leaving I saw a Mercedes park up the street and three heavy-looking Greek or Turkish blokes getting out. They walked past me and into the club.

For some reason, they had attracted my interest. Call it sixth sense if you like, but it was screaming. I wasn't sure why until I walked up the road to their car. They'd left it unlocked and on the back seat was a flash briefcase. I had a quick look about, opened the door and nabbed the case. Then I walked to the station and jumped on the Tube. When I got home I looked inside. I'd hit gold.

There was a big bag of cocaine and a few crooked passports. I never liked drugs so I phoned a mate and he took the case off my hands for a few quid, no questions asked. I bought a Mercedes myself with the dosh. Another nice little earner. Sometime later, rumours circulated through the underworld that a Turkish gang had been robbed outside Stringfellows at gunpoint, possibly by another firm. They obviously didn't want to admit they'd left the car doors open.

About that time, 'Big' Paul Foley and Danny Woollard bought a stake in a nightclub called Antics in Bow. I was having a drink there one night with Danny when the doorman, a real hard man but a thorough gent called Johnny Cooney, called us down. Two blokes were trying to get in for free, claiming they knew us.

When we saw them we realised they were trying it on. Neither of us knew them from Adam. They were beered up and spoiling for trouble. Danny really didn't want them in his club, so he said: 'Look, lads, when Paul's here you can get in for free. Until then you pay, all right?'

'You don't know who I am, mate,' came the reply from one of them.

'I don't and I don't really care,' replied Danny.

The bloke's mate added: 'Soon you'll be paying us to come in.'

That was it. 'Look, lads,' I said, 'do yourselves a favour and piss off now before you wind someone up. There are paying punters waiting to come in and you're blocking the door.'

Suddenly, one of them pulled a knife and lunged at Danny. He moved liked greased lightning, belting the bloke hard on the jaw. His mate jumped on Danny's back so I smashed him in the back of the head, then tore into him when he let go. Right. Left. Right. Until it was clear he was finished. Johnny had given the first bloke a slap after Danny. Within seconds both of them were lying in the gutter groaning, as customers stepped over them. I had barely broken a sweat. It was proof if we needed it that the mugs were getting thicker, pulling a blade on three of the canniest street fighters in London. No one gave them another glance; they knew troublemakers when they saw them.

The next day, Danny got a phone call from a friend saying the two geezers were threatening to do us both properly. It was another empty gesture. We never heard any more from either of them. At the time, London was changing. There were more guns on the streets and the violence was getting more extreme. The days when a grudge could be settled on the cobbles were nearing an end. Wannabe gangsters were getting tooled up to go to the shops for a pint of milk. Some of the older faces used this as an excuse to arm themselves more heavily but I didn't like it one bit. If I'd learned one thing, it was that violence begets violence.

Meanwhile, we were still ducking and diving, trying to make a few quid to keep the wolf from the door, not always successfully. And sometimes with the most bizarre results. Danny knew a bloke with some serious business muscle who had been made bankrupt but still had money owing to him. If the cash went into his account, it would be seized by his creditors, so he was looking for someone to accept a £50,000 cheque on his behalf. When it was cashed, he'd take £35,000, leaving £15,000 to be split three ways between Danny, myself and whoever we could get to accept the cheque and the risk of a money-laundering charge.

We couldn't take it – we were too hot with the cops – so I rang a shady accountant I knew. He was as sharp as a razor and familiar with every trick in the book. Within a week, he'd found a likely candidate, one Mr Berge who lived in a nice house in Buckinghamshire. I checked him out and he seemed honest, so the cheque was signed in his name and we sat back to wait 10 days for it to be cashed.

Unbeknown to us, however, Mr Berge had some financial problems of his own, the most pressing being a £4,000 debt to some nasty fellas who were getting impatient. He had intended to pay his debt with the £5,000 he got from us. But they wouldn't wait. The next thing, a bloke called Big Lonny, a huge bodybuilder, turned up with a mate on Mr Berge's front porch demanding the cash. They'd been hired as debt collectors for 10 per cent of the total. It was getting complicated.

Mr Berge was an ordinary bloke so he invited Big Lonny and his mate in to explain the situation. This Lonny was a maniac; he thought Mr Berge was giving him the runaround and went mad. He started screaming at the poor bloke and his wife – 'No one fucks with Big Lonny' – and scared him witless. Mr Berge promised the money the next day, but that wasn't enough for Big Lonny.

He said, 'I'm coming back tomorrow for the money. You'd better find it from somewhere. In the meantime, I'll give you something to think about, and this is only a taste of what you'll get if you don't cough up our cash.'

He grabbed Mr Berge, bent him over a table and pulled down his trousers and pants. Then, while his pal held him down, Lonny shoved a stick of Ralgex muscle relief up the poor bloke's jacksy as he screamed in agony and terror. I think his wife probably passed out with the shock. Like I said, they were ordinary folk.

I got a call from my accountant mate and drove to Mr Berge's house with Danny as fast as we could. When we got there, he was in bed and his wife was still in a terrible state of shock. She must've been around 35, but she had aged 20 years and looked like she had been crying for a week. I tried to calm her down and told her I'd go and sort out this Big Lonny. She gave me his phone number and I rang him up in front of her. When he answered he asked what he could do for me. I replied: 'No, mate, it's what I can do for you. I'm at Mr Berge's house and I've picked up some money for you. Come to our office tomorrow.'

He was thrilled. I told Mr Berge's wife it was sorted. This bloke would be off their back and they could relax.

The next day, I was waiting with Danny at his office. At 10am on the button, the bell rang and two giants walked in. Big Lonny's nickname was spot on: he was truly huge. His mate wasn't quite as tall but he was as wide as a garage door and built like a house. They looked a formidable pair.

I said, 'Look, Lonny, we've got an ongoing deal with Mr Berge and I've got to collect some money off him myself in a couple of days. You're messing it up.'

'I don't care,' he replied, 'you said you've got my money, so where is it? This had better not be a waste of my time.'

'OK, here it is,' I said, handing him a piece of paper.

Written on it was: 'IOU £4,000 – Micky Glückstad'.

'Is this a fucking joke?' he stormed.

'No, Lonny,' I replied, looking him square in the eye. 'My credit's good everywhere. If you can wait two days you'll have your money once we've been paid.'

The other geezer had stayed silent up until then. Now he jumped up and said: 'Lonny, these blokes think we're fucking mugs.'

It was about to kick off, so I snatched a bottle of ammonia from my pocket and squirted him straight in the face. He went down screaming and I lunged across the desk and smacked him a couple of times so he got the message.

Big Lonny was on his feet, bellowing like a bull and lashing out at Danny and myself. Dan hit him straight on the jaw and he went down, throwing a couple of wild swings as he fell. I could see Lonny was in trouble. He was gasping for breath and I thought he might be going to die. Maybe the ammonia fumes had affected him. I rushed round the desk and dragged him on to his feet then stuck him on a chair.

After a few minutes, he was able to breathe again. I said, 'Look, Lonny, you should see someone about that chest of yours, mate.'

'No, I've got flu, that's all,' he wheezed.

'Listen,' I continued, 'there was no need for that at all. I'll give you your money fair and square in two days' time.'

Lonny agreed and left, taking his mate with him. Both of them were in a right sorry state, truth be told, but I think they had got the message.

I rang Mr Berge's wife to tell her the good news. She was in tears.

'Micky, something terrible's happened,' she told me, between sobs. 'My husband hanged himself last night in our garage.'

I was stunned. Whether it was fear of Lonny and his mate, or the humiliation of what they had done to him, we would never know for sure. One thing seemed certain; our money was gone. The £50,000 was paid into his account and swallowed up by the debts of his estate.

None of us ever saw a penny of it – not me, not Danny and certainly not Big Lonny. I rang him to tell him what had happened to Mr Berge. I've never heard a bloke more frightened. Him and his mate made themselves scarce.

* * *

A good corner job is tricking someone into paying you for goods or services you don't have, buying fresh air if you like, or tricking someone else into giving you a commodity they are trying to sell without your paying for it. Basically, it works both ways, but the genius is in the trickery. The corner job is a confidence job above all else. If you've got the confidence, you'll have the customer.

A perfect example was when a friend gave me the number of a fella who wanted to do some business. He'd heard I could get hold of snide £20 notes. Apart from my disastrous foray into printing years earlier, I'd never had any time for the forgery game. I had no idea why the bloke thought I was the man to help him. But I jumped at the chance to earn some cash. I phoned him up and told him I knew a man who could help him. I'd act as third party for a small fee and deliver the goods. They'd cost him £3 each, giving him a handsome profit, and they were good, so good no one would guess they were forgeries. He was in. We met the next day at a petrol station in Dartford and I gave him five £20 notes to inspect. He was impressed.

'These are amazing, Micky,' he told me, holding them up against the light to inspect the watermarks and silver strip.

They should be, I thought. I'd got them brand new from my local bank that very morning.

'Yeah, they're good,' I replied. 'There are five different serial numbers as you can see and these will pass any test. My man can print on demand.'

He gave me £15 for the notes and we agreed to meet in a week or so while my mate sorted the printing. He phoned me the next day. 'Mick, they're really good. I tried them out and no one clocked them as fake. I want to buy 10 grand's worth of your notes as soon as possible. Can you deliver?'

'Sure I can.'

I didn't want to make it too easy, or I thought he might get suspicious. So I arranged a meeting at Mile End station the following week. I made him drive and directed him to pull in by a block of flats in Plaistow.

'Got the money?'

He handed me an envelope stuffed with £50 notes. Remembering the time I'd been stiffed by the Irish bloke for his non-existent guns, I counted every last note. It was all there. I could feel my blood rising in anticipation of the con.

'OK, pal,' I said, 'the merchandise is inside.'

I started to get out of the car and he went to follow me.

'No, mate, you wait here. No one can come into his flat. He's terrified about being nicked – he's just come out of a 10-year stretch.'

'OK, Mick, I understand,' he said and got back into his car.

I gave him a wave and walked towards the flats. The security system was broken but I made a show of pressing a button and waiting for a reply. I gave it about a minute, then walked in with a final wave. Inside, I checked the bundle of notes was safe and sound inside my jacket, then hurried out the back door of the building. I'd left my car there earlier, so I jumped in and drove off, leaving the bloke waiting outside the front.

The next day I called him. He was spitting feathers.

'What the fuck happened, Micky?' he demanded. 'I want my notes or my money. You're trying it on.'

'Just a fucking minute, mate,' I shouted back, 'hear me out. I've just got out of the nick after spending the night locked up. Undercover CID were waiting for me inside the flat yesterday. Did you tell anyone about this deal because they seemed to know a lot. Are you an undercover cop?'

Now he was on the back foot and seriously shitting himself.

'Hang on, Mick,' he said. 'I never told a single soul. That's the truth. And I'm not police, either. I just want my money back and we'll call it quits. You didn't tell them about me, did you?'

'Well, they seemed to know a fuck of a lot, that's all I know,' I continued. 'I kept my mouth shut so you're in the clear but they've confiscated your dough. You're going to have to live with that because there's no chance of them giving it back, no matter how nicely I ask. And I haven't got any cash. I'll be lucky if I don't get five years for this. Turning up at a forger's flat with 10 grand in my pocket.'

He went quiet at that, and I knew I had him now.

'Look,' I said, 'my mate's been nicked. He's fucked too, but I know someone else who might be able to do you a deal. I'm not getting involved this time though. It's already cost me too much. Call me if you want me to set you up.'

I slammed down the phone and never heard from him again. After I'd written off the £100 I'd splashed, I'd made £9,900 profit minus some petrol money. As good a week's work as there ever was.

A month later, I was drinking by myself when in walked a bloke called Willie Ward. He was from Glasgow and a proper hard man, with a furious scar down the side of his face from his eye to his chin where he'd been slashed. I knew him by reputation but we got talking and he was a lovely bloke. He told me his mate had taken over a pub in Upton Park, near West Ham FC, and he was going to help run it on match days. I knew the area well – it was like the Wild West when there was a big game – and I thought it would definitely be worth the taxi ride next time the Hammers were at home to see Willie at work.

It was worth it. He soon got a name as 'One Punch' Willie Ward, and knocked many a muppet out cold with a single punch. His reputation grew fast, maybe too fast, and he was soon known around the East End as a proper hard man. That brought him to the attention of the cops. And before long, he was making the journey back to Glasgow. We stayed in touch and I fully expect to read his story one of these days. No doubt it'll be a cracker.

There was still good money to be made on the unlicensed boxing circuit and Danny, who had married a traveller, Beccy, was very well connected. I needed some cash so he sorted me some prizefights in gypsy camps around the country. The first was in Southampton. I won easily. I can't recall much about my opponent now, but he was easy meat and went down quickly for a gypsy. The second fight, in Kent, was a real tear-up but I won again. I hadn't lost my instincts for battle, that much was obvious, and I enjoyed it.

The last fight Danny had arranged was in Liverpool against a Greek gypsy who came with a huge reputation. I think he called himself the Gypsy Champion of the World or something similar. I went into the ring confidently but this man was dynamite. He came straight at me, no messing about. Before I could raise my fists I'd been punched into the next day with a flurry of blows to my head and body. I staggered back, only just managing to keep on my feet.

He was piling blows into my ribs and I couldn't stop him. It didn't take long for him to punch me out of the ring. In a long career fighting, I never met anyone I didn't think I could've bested in a street fight, except this man, whoever he was. It was a terrific battle but he knocked me stupid. I lost the fight but I lost it well. Afterwards, as was usual, we shared a proper drink. There was still a lot of respect.

I didn't know it then, but that was my last gypsy fight.